COMMUNICATING FOR PRODUCTIVITY

CONTINUING MANAGEMENT EDUCATION SERIES

Under the Advisory Editorship of Albert W. Schrader

COMMUNICATING FOR PRODUCTIVITY

ROGER D'APRIX

Consultant, Towers, Perrin, Forster & Crosby
formerly manager of employee communication,
Xerox Corporation

HarperCollins*Publishers*

Executive Editor: Fred Henry
Project Editor: Rita Williams
Designer: T. R. Funderburk
Production Manager: Jeanie Berke
Compositor: ComCom Division of Haddon Craftsmen, Inc.
Printer and Binder: R. R. Donnelley & Sons Company
Art Studio: Vantage Art, Inc.

Communicating for Productivity

Copyright © 1982 by Roger D'Aprix

Library of Congress Cataloging in Publication Data

D'Aprix, Roger M.
    Communicating for productivity.
    (Continuing management education series)
    Includes index.
    1. Communication in management. I. Title. II. Series.
HD30.3.D36   658.4′5   82-1108
ISBN 0-06-041547-9   AACR2

For the people who matter most in my life—
my best friend and lifelong partner, Theresa;
our first-born and always special daughter, Cynthia;
our dreamer and marcher to a different drum, Richard;
our giver (and sharer of other's joys and woes), Laura;
and our bonus child and joy of our middle years, Tony.

Contents

Foreword

In the face of inflation, the energy crisis, and strong international business competition, a worrisome question is what can be done to spur human productivity. The problem of human productivity is a difficult and complex one; the causes lie in a tangle of events and past mistakes.

Whatever its causes, however, I believe that one of the most important things we need to do to begin dealing with human productivity is to enlist the support and cooperation of the people who work for our various institutional organizations. To date, we haven't done that in any systematic or effective way. In fact, we have generally relegated human communication in most of our organizations to happenstance.

For years I've sensed a contagious defeatism when it comes to making a full-scale assault on the problem. Those of us in the communication profession, as well as our professional colleagues in such human resource specialties as training, organization development, management development, and day-to-day personnel functions, prefer to look only at our particular aspect of the problem. I think I understand why. There is no working model in any organization we can point to (other than perhaps the Japanese model) and modify for our own purposes. Further, I believe that many of us are uneasy about how our management will react to any human productivity proposals that offer grandiose schemes for coordinating information programs, human resource programs, and even hint at the need to change the corporate culture we have constructed. All of this seems scary simply because it looks so revolutionary and untried.

Yet there are some commonsense things that we can do to begin dealing with the need to improve human productivity. In my mind, one of the most commonsense things of all of these is to communicate about it—to help the members of institutional organizations understand the nature of the problem, its importance to them, and what they can do to help.

At the same time, we will have to change the way we perceive and treat our human resources. Even the term "human resources" will eventually have to go because it suggests that people are like any of the other resources an organization "owns," as though they are inventory of a sort that depreciates and can be written off the books some day.

This book proposes a whole new way of looking at organizational communication. It treats organizational communication as an integral part of the process of managing and dealing with people. It takes communication from the category of "afterthought" and makes it part of the organization's business strategy. Ultimately, it recognizes that the success of this strategy is dependent on people's understanding, commitment, and creativity.

Ironically, one person who has some strong feelings about the subject of American productivity is Akio Morita, the chairman and cofounder of Sony Corporation. Because Sony has operated in both Japan and the United States and because Morita has become a man of two cultures—Japanese and American—his views of what is currently amiss in American industry are worth heeding. In a recent interview in the *New York Times Magazine,* Morita was critical of American management on two scores: "American managers are too concerned about short-term profits and too little concerned about their workers. . . . Teamwork historically . . . is the American way," Morita says. "But your managers too often forget that. . . . They viewed the worker as a tool. That has not been good for American products or American companies, and it has hurt your competitive stature in the world."[1]

Jerome Rosow, president of the Work in America Institute, Incorporated, and a leading expert on productivity, puts it a little differently. He says, "The investment of capital and the introduction of new technology each plays a part in boosting productivity, but the human resources of the organization—employees in every occupation and at every level—are clearly at the heart of any effort."[2]

What follows in this book is a prescription for an employee communication strategy to address the vital question of how we can communicate to influence and improve human productivity.

Acknowledgments

No book ever belongs exclusively to an author. It is the product of the author's mind, but the raw material—the experience—comes from a multitude of sources and places.

[1]Steve Lehr, "Overhauling America's Business Management," *New York Times Magazine,* January 4, 1981, p. 17.

[2]Jerome Rosow, "Productivity and People," an address to the 1980 Annual Seminar of the Industrial Communication Council, Chicago, October 1980.

It would be impossible for me to cite by name all the people who have directly or indirectly contributed to this work. My professional affiliations and my work at Xerox Corporation brought me into contact with some brilliant people who have nurtured my personal and professional growth in communication. These professionals' suggestions, challenges, ideas, and, sometimes, skepticism have all shaped my attitudes about organizational communication.

I would like to believe that I am the instrument for communicating their truths as well as my own. The wisdom in this book, then, is collective. The flaws are the product of my own limitations.

I was fortunate to be a part of as progressive and innovative an organization as the Xerox Corporation. My experience with Xerox remains the source of much of my hope for the ability of contemporary organizations to accommodate to today's rate of change. Still, I should make the emphatic point that this book should not be construed to have the endorsement or approval of Xerox. It is wholly a personal statement of my view of organizational communication.

The people whose support I would like to single out by name are my own family. My wife Theresa and my four children—Cynthia, Richard, Laura, and Tony—have been supportive throughout the ordeal of preparing a manuscript for publication. Without that support, you simply don't get to write books, particularly when such writing must be done at night and at the expense of family needs and activities. For my family's indulgence and interest, I offer my sincere thanks.

Roger D'Aprix

COMMUNICATING FOR PRODUCTIVITY

Chapter 1

The Care and Feeding of Alligators

The classic office cartoon of the seventies was a crude illustration of a harried man standing in a swamp and surrounded by menacing alligators. The caption reads, "It's hard to remember that you're supposed to drain the swamp when you're up to your ass in alligators."

That cartoon is displayed in thousands of offices and work areas throughout the United States as a statement of how people feel about their work lives. It is also, incidentally, a graphic statement of the position most work organizations find themselves in today.

Hostility to large organizations is certainly not a new phenomenon in American life. Anyone who remembers the cowboy epics in which the uncaring railroad was swindling yet another settler out of his hard-earned landholdings knows that. The difference lies in the extent and intensity of this hostility.

More particularly, it stems from two important changes in American society in the last generation. The first change is that more of us than ever before are dependent on large organizations for our living. The fate of most people in American society is to work in and for some sort of institutional organization that is bigger and more powerful than they are—either individually or as a group. It is a rare soul who achieves this insight, counts his blessings, and gushes forth his undying appreciation. The more typical reaction is to cast an uneasy eye at the railroad and to wonder what the land agents are up to this time.

The second change is more complex. It is the changing expectations American workers are bringing to the work place. Better educated, more sophisticated, and equipped with a longer list of needs, wants, and demands, today's workers expect much more from the job than did their parents or grandparents.

In large measure, the first change has led us as a society to worry about whether our organizations are up to the challenges that face them in the years ahead. Inflation, energy shortages, some shifts in the world's wealth, the emerging power and muscle flexing of oil rich nations—all these have combined with other anxieties to cause us to doubt that our institutional leaders are perceptive enough and wise enough to drain the swamp before the alligators overtake them—and us.

This latter change has led us to a generalized restlessness and alienation. *I* want satisfaction. *I* want fulfillment. *I* want recognition. *I* want security. *I* want someone to care, and on and on.

Many of today's organizational leaders feel besieged by hostile forces. Adding to and compounding the concerns of the work force are the cries of alarm and distrust from the media, government, and university community. It is small wonder that institutional leaders—and business leaders in particular—feel unloved and bewildered.

To a large extent they are trapped in their own myths. For years organizational leaders said to the public and to one another that organizations are efficient, well managed, and intelligent; that they exist for the benefit of their employees, owners, and customers; that they objectively reward dedication, competence, and performance; and that they are dynamic and receptive to change. This was the institutional credo on which most of us were reared. And during the fifties and early sixties, it seemed eminently correct and truthful.

Certainly during the go-go years of the soaring sixties, when business leaders were collecting the kudos and dollars of eager investors and searching hungrily for other companies to acquire, it all seemed to make good sense. But events have shown the corporate credo to be more ideal than real, more aspiration than truth. The aspirations were not bad by any means but were bound to lead to disillusionment when the going got heavy.

Today, most Americans are skeptical and more than a little angry about the performance of institutional organizations. The leaders of these organizations are becoming more and more aware of this anger and want very much to do something, but the truth is that most of the leaders don't know what to do.

This book focuses on one critical facet of this very vexing problem: how institutional management can win the understanding and support of its single most important constituency—its employees. The simple premise is that organizations must put their own houses in order before they can attempt to gain the support of any other constituency.

That is not an easy task, because institutional leaders, like neglectful husbands and fathers, are in trouble at home. They have taken for granted the people they were supposed to love most, whom the annual reports all described as "our most valued resource." The problem is that employees didn't read the annual reports, or if they did, they didn't believe them. What they believed was their day-to-day experience—which is what people always believe.

A traditional institutional belief that is seldom articulated, but which defeats most of our attempts at enlightened management and even at effective management training, is the notion of the divine right of kings—that somehow God has ordained institutional authority. Most managers really believe that there are only two ways to manage people. On the one hand, you can be tough-minded and demanding and manage through threats and punishments that are balanced with rewards for compliance. On the other, you can be soft and permissive and finally allow the inmates to run the asylum. In that case, the result most likely will be chaos, and ultimate failure.

When the premise is stated that baldly, most enlightened managers will object and claim that they do not believe any such thing. Yet when these managers' on-the-job behavior is examined, it is difficult to resist the conclusion that they are operating from the position of ruler or parent in their dealings with the people who report to them.

It is not difficult to understand why there are monumental employee morale and employee communication problems in practically all work organizations. Our collective dependence on organizations for a livelihood, our increasing expectations of the satisfaction work can provide, management's tendency to invoke the corporate credo when questioned or criticized, and a divine-right faith in the obligation of people in positions of authority to dole out punishment all combine to defeat our efforts to improve management practice and organizational understanding.

Management desperately needs spokesmen and spokeswomen to articulate its positions and attitudes. Theoretically, the most logical people to perform this task would be the organization's line managers—supervisors, foremen, middle managers—but no one ever told them that this responsibility came with the territory. Not only were they not told, they were also not trained.

Although we have not told managers that effective interpersonal communication was a major part of their responsibilities, we have made it clear that they were responsible for results.

In particular, managers were to deliver quality products on time and at a profit. And they were to stay at or under budget. Nothing else mattered very much, at least in the measurement of their performance. When it came to the people they managed, the conventional wisdom was not to get involved. Above all else the line managers were expected to remain objective in their relationships (although that sounds to me like a contradiction) so that they could be objective in their evaluation.

The manager in many of our large institutional organizations is now being asked to speak for his or her own management. Most of them don't like the role very much and are prepared to duck it wherever and whenever possible.

Author Michael Maccoby in his best-seller *The Gamesman* claims that we have actually created our own institutional Frankensteins who have learned to repress their emotions and to focus on life and work as a game in which all that counts is winning. Such managers learn in time to silence any personal inclination toward compassion or concern for the people who are the victims of their game plans.¹ The best analogy is probably the general sending troops into combat. If he cares too much about the casualties, he soon becomes a timid general. So it is with gamesmen.

In part this is merely a logical extension of the American tradition of admiring the rough, tough individualist, the self-made person who asks and gives no quarter. That is an important part of our folklore, but as our various institutions become more complex and interrelated, this view of life becomes less and less appropriate.

Without belaboring the point, it might be useful to contrast the operating style of a traditional American organization with its Japanese counterpart.² In general, the American organization makes no promises about employment longevity. The assumption usually is that one has a job for an indefinite period, but American workers are accustomed to the specter of layoffs and to the knowledge that if things get bad enough, their jobs may well be in jeopardy. The Japanese tradition is lifetime employment, with emphasis on the mutual responsibility of employer and employee.

There is also greater emphasis on individual responsibility in an American company. The Japanese tend to focus on collective responsibility. Along with that goes the tendency in the United States to make decision making the province of individuals. In Japan there is greater stress on decision making by consent of the group.

The American organization typically emphasizes rapid evaluation and promotion. Here, too, the Japanese tend to be more patient and to evaluate performance over a longer span of time—say, 5 or 10 years in contrast to the typical 12-month performance cycle in the United States.

Another important difference is that U.S. companies have specialized career paths with a high degree of professionalization.

In turn, that naturally leads to career rather than organizational loyalty. In fact, that degree of specialization ironically increases mobility from organization to organization, since skills become quite portable. In Japan, career paths tend to be nonspecialized, with the result that loyalty to the organization tends to increase and career loyalty tends to decrease.

Finally, one of the most important differences—particularly insofar as it affects the communication process—is the degree of concern felt for the individual. In the United States, this concern is usually confined to the immediate work situation in the belief that any employee's problems outside work are strictly up to him or her to resolve. The important thing is to be at work every day and to give a fair day's work.

In Japan, on the other hand, managers are expected to know the personal circumstances of each of their subordinates and to be concerned with them as whole people.

Relationships in an American organization are purposely more casual. We have trained our managers to maintain their objectivity so that they could evaluate performance with a certain degree of emotional distance from the people they are measuring. American managers have been conditioned to repress their emotions and not get involved with subordinates.

The all-too-typical picture in most U.S. corporate organizations is an obsessive emphasis on "the numbers" at the expense of practically any other value, human or otherwise. The inevitable result in such an environment is a devaluing of human relationships.

It's the great obscenity of organization life, one we deal with by pretending it doesn't exist. In *The Gamesman,* Maccoby says people simply repress their normal feelings.[3] Sadly, that kind of repression at work leads them to do the same in their relationships outside the work place. For the individual the loss of this human dimension is tragic.

For the organization, the toll is demotivation and ineffective and nonexistent communication, and the undermining of any sense of team spirit or concern is catastrophic. Because that toll cannot be appraised in any objective way, management frequently loses sight of it or claims that nothing can be done about it.

I have even heard some managers argue that if you worry about such things, you will somehow undermine the organization's will to compete. It's as if a supportive and concerned work environment would destroy people's will to work.

Certainly the experience of the Japanese in earning the intense worker loyalty for which they have become famous contradicts that view. Japanese productivity and Japanese innovation and competitiveness suggest that we could take some lessons in this country in the art of motivating employees.

A look at a fictional American company, Excello Business Machines,* may illustrate some of the ways that large business organizations get themselves into trouble with their work force. Excello is a fairly typical growth company spawned in the early 1960s by a group of engineers and marketing specialists who left their Fortune 500 electronics company to concentrate on the manufacture and sale of office accessories. It was especially successful in the manufacture of pocket calculators when such devices were still a novelty item. This early success, and the growth it brought to the company, encouraged the belief that Excello management was shrewd and perceptive. No one believed this more devoutly than the senior staff of Excello.

The result was that a casual management style developed in the business, with a good deal of shooting from the hip. This style had worked beautifully in the case of the pocket calculator, originally a low-priority product that took off as soon as it was introduced. This success persuaded Excello management that they were indeed a shrewd group of entrepreneurs.

Since they had come from the electronics business with extensive experience in specialized computer design, they decided to go after a share of the computer

---

*Excello and the other case histories I cite here are products of my imagination. Any resemblance to real American companies—either living or dead—is purely coincidental.

market. The group market research data was scanty at best; its ability to plan and orchestrate the manufacture and sale of the terminals in an office environment was marginal. This was compounded by the bewildering stagflation of the 1970s, and in short order Excello was caught in severe cash flow problems.

The brightest and cleverest of the Excello executives had always been the founder and prime mover, the president of the company, Phil Noble. As soon as he recognized the possibility of a market disaster, he hired one of the country's leading management consultants to assess the fix Excello was in and to recommend a course of action. The consultant's verdict was that the company could recover and perhaps even prosper in this business if it attended to basics and if it could somehow get its burgeoning costs under control. In the consultant's considered opinion, a large chunk of the company's overhead had to be lopped off to avert disaster.

Noble knew that his senior staff was not up to the kind of discipline and tough decisions that faced the company, so he eased out three of his key staff people and replaced them with experienced executives from more traditional and better-disciplined companies. The decision was unpopular with Excello middle managers especially, who resented outsiders having been brought into the business to block their future career moves.

The resulting changes went far beyond what anyone dreamed they might be in the beginning of this shake-up. Eventually 5,000 of the company's 20,000 employees were laid off as the cost cutting process chewed away at the fat that Excello management had permitted the company to take on. Organizations were reorganized, consolidated, and, when possible, eliminated. Manufacturing, sales, and service were all scrutinized with the greatest emphasis put on long-range analysis and planning. New techniques were developed to improve productivity and capture cost savings in every major department.

The entire process took Excello three years to complete. By the time the dust had settled, Excello was an efficient organization that knew how to plan and manage the business better than at any time in its history.

Despite its success, however, there was an undercurrent of employee distrust and distress as a legacy of the cost and employee reduction efforts. Harry Waddell, Excello's vice-president and director of personnel, commissioned the Attitude Research Corporation to do an extensive attitude survey of Excello employees to determine their concerns and to see how they stacked up against a similar survey that had been done at Excello five years earlier.

In every single category of the survey, there was marked erosion of attitudes from the earlier study. Employees were much less confident about the future than they had been. They worried that Excello management still might not be able to develop workable strategy for the present or future.

They were especially concerned about competition both in the United States and overseas. They wanted reassurances that their own management understood the threat and was doing something. So far, they claimed, they did not see much evidence of that. What was in the product pipeline? What was the strategy to keep

Excello competitive after the trauma of the severe cutbacks? What was the likelihood of future cutbacks?

The whole survey was shot through with a clear distrust of Excello management—their competence, motives, and concern for the welfare of Excello people. First-level managers were regarded as more trustworthy, but they were also seen as relatively powerless. It was clear that Excello people were restless and resentful. But the good news was that they still cared what happened to the company. They wanted the company to be successful, and they wanted to contribute to that success.

Those aspirations were certainly supported by Excello management, but they were disconcerted by the negative findings. One by one they conducted their own informal inquiries to determine if there was any basis to the survey results. In the process they got an earful. Judging from the informal feedback, the survey was *understating* the severity of the problem, or so management began to think from their conversations with small groups of employees.

When the Excello senior staff met to discuss an action plan, they could only agree that there was a problem.

What to do about that problem was a matter of considerable disagreement. Solutions ranged all the way from developing a massive program to react to employee discontent to the proposal of at least one staff officer that the best thing to do would be to pretend the survey had never been taken. The lack of consensus predictably led to paralysis and indecision, and six months passed without any visible reaction to the survey. Although it was hardly a ground swell, there were many employee questions about the survey and what became of it.

In the meantime the hourly production force began to show some alarming signs of discontent. Excello had bid and lost on a major government contract for a time-sharing system. It was common knowledge that this contract had been counted on by Excello marketing people to meet this year's ambitious marketing plan. When Excello's proposal was rejected, the grapevine began circulating the rumor that layoffs were inevitable. The layoffs were scheduled, said the grapevine, for the next month and would be based on a policy of weeding out the higher-paid, more senior people first so that the greatest cost savings could be realized.

In this atmosphere of uncertainty the local organizer of the Association of Electrical Workers began making overtures to some of the more dissatisfied among the production people. Soon they were agitating with their fellow workers about the need for a union to protect Excello people against Excello management.

Immediately, Waddell delegated his human relations manager, Pete Rizzo, to find out what was happening and to quell the rumors. Rizzo, who was a former foreman and who was trusted by the production people, did an outstanding job of calming people and persuading them that there was no substance to the messages being spread by the grapevine.

But Rizzo came back to his own management with a warning that they had better address the concerns and anxieties of Excello people and pay attention to what the survey had told them. In his judgment, if they didn't, there would be a union to deal with. He also believed that when the economy turned upward there could well be a mass exodus from Excello of professional people who were fed up with the pressure and the insensitivity of management.

Among American business organizations today the Excello case is not unusual. Speaking about real companies, Dr. Michael Cooper says there is "a hierarchy gap." He claims that 90–95 percent of managers studied in 159 organizations over 25 years are satisfied with their jobs. But for both hourly and clerical workers, job satisfaction is the lowest ever.

The reasons for this condition are instructive. A majority of the unhappy workers stated that their companies do not treat them with respect as individuals. They are seen instead as numbers, as company inventory. Cooper concludes that these people, in keeping with the expectations of the 1960s and 1970s, believe they should experience some intrinsic satisfaction from their work.

Further, Cooper states that only 28 percent of hourly employees rated their companies as "very good" or "good" in letting them know what was going on in the business. That figure is down significantly from the 1950s, when 43 percent gave management good marks on this item.

On the matter of whether the company cared to listen to their concerns, over 70 percent expressed their skepticism that management cared or would do anything.[4] So Excello is far from an isolated case.

The question is what American institutional organizations can do to address this kind of wholesale loss of confidence and mistrust. It's a fascinating question —and one screaming for an answer if American private enterprise is to remain healthy and competitive in the years ahead.

A good starting point in searching for an answer is perhaps to see what morals can be drawn from Excello's experience. There are several employee communication lessons to be learned in the way Excello has approached its problems. The first is a fundamental of organization communication. It is so fundamental that it would seem unnecessary even to state it. But it is a lesson management ignores over and over again in its dealings with the work force: one's actions *always* drown out one's words.

Management can say as much as it wants in whatever media it chooses that "our employees are our most valuable resource." If it says this from one side of its mouth and then from the other orders a layoff as its first action when the going gets tough, then employees correctly decline to believe the words. If people are not treated well, if they are watched and clearly not trusted, if they are never given any feedback except in the form of haranguing or criticism, then they will believe their experience and ignore the fair words.

It never ceases to amaze me that so many managers decline to accept this fundamental of good communication. Instead, they continue to look for someone who can magically excuse and explain their behavior to the people whom they have wronged. So lesson number one is that good communication is impossible without management consistently, and to the best of their ability, doing the right thing according to the dictates of the problem or situation they are dealing with.

Excello employees are unhappy because they took it on the chin for a blundering and inexperienced management. Of the 5000 people who were laid off in the overhead reductions before the attitude survey, not one person was from the senior management ranks of the company, except for the three who were eased into other jobs when the purge first began. Is it any wonder that the employees are anxious and distrustful?

Lesson number two is that the employees of an organization do not automatically identify their interests with the interests of that organization. When a company is doing well or even when it appears that it may do poorly, employees sometimes have difficulty seeing what stake they have in all that. This is particularly true when the organization is having a streak of business successes. It does not necessarily follow that employees will be applauding management for its wisdom and careful management of resources.

Excello, for example, after the layoffs and reshuffling, was doing very well financially. Employees, on the other hand, were unhappy and resentful.

Lesson number three is that employees have multiple sources of information. They are not totally—or even mainly—dependent on what they are told through official channels. Employees' most trusted information source is their own day-to-day experience. Excello people could see what was happening both in the marketplace and within the company, and they speculated freely about the consequences. They also read the newspapers and watched television and had access generally to what others thought about the business and its prospects.

And, of course, there is the ever-present grapevine. At Excello it is a well-developed medium that is fed often by the people in a position to know bits and pieces of what is happening as those bits and pieces surface. It is generally accurate, although incomplete and unofficial. The result is that people eagerly seek information from the grapevine at the same time that they resent having to resort to it to find out what is happening in their company.

Lesson number four from Excello's plight is this: don't ask people their opinions and suggestions if you really don't care to respond to them. The survey was informative and potentially useful as a diagnostic tool to determine an appropriate action program. But the patient must be given both a diagnosis *and* a treatment plan before he or she has much confidence in the doctor. If the doctor declines to give the diagnosis—or, worse yet, declines to treat the illness—the patient gives up hope and soon refuses to have anything at all to do with the doctor, who is obviously a quack anyway.

Lesson number five is that events such as Excello experienced will ultimately lead to some kind of employee rage, manifesting itself at various points in the organization. It may be a union campaign. It may be a drop in productivity. It can even be sabotage, but you can bet that somehow, somewhere, people who feel wronged will find a way to express their feelings to the detriment of the organization.

There are undoubtedly other lessons, but these are the major ones for us who favor alligator watching. In the next chapter, let's see if there are systematic ways to tame the alligators so that we can go about the original task of draining the swamp.

NOTES

1. Michael Maccoby, *The Gamesman* (New York: Simon and Schuster, 1976), pp. 98–120.
2. William G. Ouchi and Alfred M. Jaeger, "Type Z Organization: A Corporate Alternative to Village Life," *Stanford Business School Alumni Bulletin*, Fall 1977–1978, pp. 13–17.
3. Maccoby, *The Gamesman*, pp. 98–120.
4. M. R. Cooper, B. S. Morgan, P. M. Foley, and L. B. Kaplan, "Changing Employee Values: Deepening Discontent?" *Harvard Business Review*, January–February 1979, pp. 117–125.

Chapter 2

Organizational Communication: Some Emerging Trends

If we are going to improve the communication process in our various organizations, we must come to grips with some fundamentals early in our discussion. First, the employee audience. What does it want? Second, management. What must they be prepared to do and how must they do it? Third, considering these needs and demands, what should be the priorities for any management honestly wanting to do better in communication?

These are not easy questions. In fact, they are the rocks on which many well-intentioned communication plans eventually founder.

The evidence from the research done on the subject indicates that employees generally have three communication needs. They want to know where the organization is heading and how it will get there and—most important—what all that means to them. The logic of the employees' needs is clear. Employees understand that their individual well-being and their very futures are tied closely to the overall success of the work organization. As members of the enterprise, they want to know generally what the battle plan is, what strategy has been worked out to make that plan work, and how hard they will have to fight to do what actually has been charted for the organization.

Although they have plenty of experience to show otherwise from their daily responsibilities, most employees believe in "the plan in the lower right-hand desk drawer of the president." That belief complicates management's communication task because it presumes that all this has been programmed in some detail and is being deliberately withheld so that management can release it a snippet at a time when it is good and ready to do so.

The truth is that most managements aren't nearly that clever in their planning. What they do most of the time is to react to the latest events and communicate them defensively and apologetically as it becomes necessary. More about this phenomenon later.

My experience tells me employees mainly want to know about the business issues that are driving the organization hither and yon. They want to have those issues defined and interpreted for them. And they want to know generally what management is prepared to do to resolve them. Note that I said "generally." One excuse offered by many managements for not communicating this kind of information is their fear that it will fall into the hands of the competition. That's mostly nonsense, because people are not asking for detailed strategic plans. All they want is some assurance that there *is* a strategy. Once they believe that, they will settle for only the broadest outline—what any competitor worthy of the name has long since figured out anyway.

Besides a reasonable statement of the issues, employees have a second basic communication need. It is to be able to identify and relate to some flesh-and-blood representation of the organization. The first choice is always the boss. Survey after survey confirms that people's main source of information in the organization is the grapevine. That usually goes for managers too!

When employees are asked which source they prefer to get their information from, the grapevine is low on the list. The inevitable first choice is the boss, for the obvious reason that he or she is a trusted source, a flesh-and-blood messenger who can be questioned and presumably has the official word.

The great credibility of the grapevine is that its messages are always delivered in person by someone the recipient knows. Management, on the other hand, normally avoids human messengers on the mistaken assumption that they are too prone to filter and distort the carefully prepared message. Instead, they rely on the written word, nicely polished and perfumed, to reassure the audience that it is as wise as it looks and smells.

What does management want from the organizational communication exchange? To answer this, we have to understand the mystique most institutional organizations attempt to live by. This mystique holds that management power is a product of four things—a command structure, tight discipline, prudent (even omniscient) decision making, and timely information gathering. To some degree, management is right in its belief in these things, but it is also more than a little wrong. To understand the paradox, let's consider the pieces of the mystique one at a time.

First, consider the command structure. Most contemporary organizations are still organized like an infantry division. This means that there is a carefully constituted chain of command to insure orderly discussion and intervention. Senior leaders of such organizations are protected against untimely interruptions of their schedules or energy.

To help insure that they are protected, the offices of senior leaders are even cordoned off in impressively carpeted and furnished chambers guarded by receptionists and secretaries. Such perquisites even become part of the reward system that tells senior people that they are indeed senior. What they also do is isolate such people from contact with their fellow workers and the day-to-day reality of the work place.

For the employees, this means that their leadership becomes remote and unreachable. Like celebrities, the leaders become people the employees have heard of but who somehow don't seem real. This circumstance defeats communication by increasing personal distance and putting people even more in awe of their absentee landlords. The end product is suspicion and an inability to guess at the motives of people the employees don't know. So employees guess anyway, because they need to know, and they assign sinister causes to the events of the work place. From leader senior management goes to unscrupulous culprit.

Second, there is the pretense that the organization functions because of tight discipline. It does, but the discipline that makes the organization go is not external. It is the self-discipline that the work force musters to pay the price of surrendering its own time and energy for the good of the organization. Contrary to popular belief, we do not elicit that self-discipline by demanding it or by punishing people who decline to give it. We elicit it by coaxing it out, by earning it from trustworthy and consistent behavior.

Managers in contemporary organizations cannot manage like a platoon sergeant, simply giving orders and presuming that they will be carried out. Not even careful supervision and follow-up will insure that. More and more, it is necessary to explain to employees why an action is necessary and how it will benefit the organization and person doing the work. Authority alone no longer does the job.

That fact is resisted by many organizations. I remember clearly the senior manager of a large manufacturing company who visited me some years ago to look at our communication programs when I was at Xerox. After I had spent a long afternoon showing him programs and discussing the logic underlying those programs, he looked at me with exasperation and said, "Wasn't it all easier when they were just glad to have a job?"

This view is not an isolated one in the world of work. But it is increasingly stupid and reactionary when measured against the realities of managing today's better educated, more demanding worker who appreciates the job yet believes in options.

Third is the damaging belief that management can or must be omniscient. This belief gets translated into a dangerous corollary in many companies: mistakes are not allowed. Accountability, in turn, becomes a process of identifying and punishing anyone guilty of an error.

In the working world there has always been a keen interest in punishment. In fairness, it should be added that the punishment is rarely as bad as the folklore would have us believe. But there is in most work situations a real fear of being punished in some way if you are found responsible for an error in judgment, the waste of any company resource, or a failed program or product. Mostly, this stems from the myth of management omniscience.

It's not hard to understand why. If managers believe they must *always* be right, they do one of several things. They may become rigidly self-dependent and decline to acknowledge that anyone else might have an idea. (Usually, that's because they're afraid to take the risk of introducing the new idea into the system, so they decline even to consider it.) Or they find ways to keep the lowest-possible profile so that if anything does go wrong, no one would consider blaming them. Or they spend lots of time and memo paper building barricades to cover their rears. Or they become expert finger-pointers. Or they perform one or more variations on each of these themes.

The point is that people do make mistakes, and no organization can legislate an error-free company. Even if it finds and punishes every transgressor, no organization can eliminate mistakes. And if an organization makes that a way of life, it will frighten everyone to the point where productivity is so low that paralysis sets in.

The consequences for effective communication are equally disastrous. In such an environment the communication channels simply become flooded with "*I* didn't do it" messages. The rest of the time there is likely to be silence.

Fourth, there is the presumption that information gathering is a source of management power. We tend to believe that good decision making is a function of lots of information, the more the better. The truth is that information can be hazardous to our health—at least to our mental health. If you doubt that, consider how it feels to watch the evening news on television or to read a daily newspaper. Generally, aside from the titillation and entertainment value of watching and reading about misfortune and the decline and fall of national figures, it's a depressing experience. The main trouble is receiving bits and pieces of often contradictory information that can't be assembled into a coherent picture. Often we put the paper down or shut off the television set with feelings of anxiety and helplessness. Our malaise is information overload, and it is epidemic in our contemporary world.

Managers and workers at all company levels suffer today from information overload. Endless and often unproductive meetings, stacks of daily mail, and jangling telephones leave us bug-eyed and stupefied at the end of our day's ingestion of information. What we now call information desperately needs to be disciplined, processed, and interpreted before it can do us much good.

When the contemporary worker suffers such information overload, he or she does the natural thing and simply declines to receive any more. At that point, communication becomes close to impossible, with only the simplest messages getting through.

In a simpler world it may have been true that this quartet of command structure and status, tight discipline, error-free decision making, and information gathering was the right formula for success. It is doubtful that it is today.

We have undergone what Father Thomas McGrath of Fairfield University calls "the cultural revolution of the 1960s." Before that fateful decade, according to Father McGrath, our society operated on the basis of three crucial values—

automatic givens all institutional leadership depended on. These were a respect for authority, a willingness to give our loyalty practically unquestioningly, and an expectation that pain was a normal part of life and discipline.

Father McGrath argues that the 1960s and the cataclysmic events that came with them destroyed these three reactions as automatic responses to institutional organizations. Respect for authority, he argues, was founded on fear of punishment. Today, if people are punished, they resolve to take their revenge. They will not accept punishment as their due, and they will not respect the authority of an institution simply because it has the power to punish.

Loyalty, he points out, is today no longer automatic. There was a time when people were blindly loyal, when they would assert *my* family, right or wrong; *my* country, right or wrong; *my* church, right or wrong; and even *my* company, right or wrong. That brand of loyalty has disappeared and is being replaced by the phenomenon of loyalty first and foremost to self. Once that obligation to self is met, people make their own decisions about to whom to give loyalty and from whom to withold it.

Institutional discipline is also up for grabs, Father McGrath says. It depended on people's willingness to pay a pain price. Pain is no longer fashionable in a world that believes in instant self-gratification. Thus it is more and more difficult to ask people to sacrifice their own interests for the good of the organization, a value that organizations once heavily depended on.[1]

It is instructive to stack Father McGrath's views against the strategic quartet of hierarchical structure and status, discipline, error-free decision making, and faith in the value of information. By and large, these time-honored management values depend on employee respect for authority and fear of authority, on myopic loyalty, and on acceptance of discipline.

The collision between employee and management values that seemingly is taking place helps to account for many of today's work place problems and could well help explain why, among other reasons, we are having difficulty holding our own against international competition. Obviously, that's a complex issue, but if management and employee values are in opposition and if management insists on trying to manage according to its own values regardless, we have a serious conflict that can't help but hurt the organization visibly.

Much has been written about today's worker and how he or she is a different breed. That proposition is not hard to confirm purely through observation. People today have more formal education. They are exposed to the trauma as well as the trivia of television. They live in an increasingly complex and bewildering society in which it becomes more and more difficult to find meaning in one's existence. Under these circumstances, it is not surprising that people would begin to rely more heavily on their work for satisfaction, even for identity.

In American culture one of the first questions we pose to one another is "What do you do?" This is a code phrase that we all understand immediately. It means tell me what your work is, and I will know who you are, how valuable you are, and where you fit in society. At least, we assume that we will be able to make those judgments from that meager information. The point is that we put great stress on job satisfaction and job identity.

My father and other fathers of his generation never expected to get much satisfaction from the job. It was "just work," and one endured it as the price of making a living, getting along, or just plain surviving. Rightly or wrongly, today's work force generally wants more from the job, and if they don't find what they want, they find ways to take out their anger and disillusionment on their employer. If you doubt that, just try to deal with an apathetic representative of some organization on the telephone when you have a problem. The classic is a computer error that you are trying to get someone to rectify on your bank statement or charge account.

Not long ago, I had a bank teller rip up my withdrawal slip and deposit it in the wastebasket beside her. My offense was thinking I had more money in my account than I did and innocently trying to write a withdrawal that exceeded the balance. After she tapped on her terminal keyboard, she concluded that I was trying to defraud the bank. In disgust she tore up my withdrawal slip. I was so astonished that I stood there in a state of shock as she waved the next customer in line to her position. When I recovered, I complained to a bank officer who gave me a sympathetic look and said, "Yes, we've had trouble with her before."

I cite this example as one of the countless opportunities that disgruntled employees have for taking out their frustration and anger on the customer. And if there's no customer immediately at hand, these employees will vent that anger in some other destructive action.

What's the answer? What can management do to cope with the situation?

Father McGrath, on the basis of his experience as both a psychologist and management consultant, tells us that our only hope is to understand that the solution is managing people through "effective relationship." The clubs no longer work, and people are not blindly loyal and will rebel against anyone who tries to manage merely by virtue of his or her authority.

It is obviously one thing to say that we can and must manage through relationship. It is something else to understand what that means and to do it. Father McGrath is not the least bit hesitant to say what it means: we must manage through respect for human dignity and human worth. What's more, he uses the love relationship as a model for what we need to learn how to do to manage people more effectively.

For the hard-headed businessperson this is a difficult model, with its overtones of "being soft on people" or with romanticized notions about the noble character of people. The old ideas about "spare the rod and spoil the child" die hard. There are strong parallels between child-rearing and managing. And in fact, most of us manage about the same way we were brought up. At least, the various authority models we use have considerable influence on our own beliefs and behavior. But the fact is that management is *not* the parent and the employee is *not* the child in today's world, and any such archaic view is bound to get us in trouble if we cling to it.

Father McGrath tells today's managers that they must do four things if they hope to manage effectively in today's organization.

The first is that they must tell their people that they and their work are valuable. They must show employees by both word and action that they care about them as persons. People, Father McGrath warns us, will not be treated like subjects or property. If we try it, he says, "They will get us." And anyone who has ever worked anywhere knows that there are subtle and almost undetectable ways to get the boss if people are so inclined.

Besides telling people of their value and importance, Father McGrath says the new manager must be prepared to give service. That's a very different role from our traditional view of the manager as a sort of nobleman who derived his power from the king and from divine right. Such a traditional manager believed that he had allegiance coming to him by virtue of his office. He believed that others should serve him.

In today's working world, the manager, asserts McGrath, must give service to others. The manager's role is to clear away the obstacles to doing the job so that people can be as productive as possible. It is a role of service and support for the people who do the work, for the truth is that managers don't do work. Managers facilitate work and get it done through others. Indeed, none of the productive work of any organization is done above the supervisory level. Under those circumstances, it is silly to have workers serving the needs of managers. It clearly must be the other way around.

This in no way diminishes the role or status of the manager. It merely changes it. The crucial question for the new manager becomes "What can I do to help you do your job better?"

Some experts believe that this change is so profound that as many as one-third of today's managers, who have become accustomed to an authoritarian view of themselves as enforcers and inspectors, will not be able to function in this kind of world. If that's so, the transition to a different way of managing people will not be an easy one, and for some it will be impossible.

The third task that McGrath says the new manager will have to learn how to perform sincerely and well is giving attention to the individual needs of the people in the organization. He likens this to the need of people in a love relationship to touch one another as a sign of their special relationship. So a manager must learn what are appropriate "touches" with his or her people. With one person it may be a sympathetic ear when things are obviously not going well. With another, it may be a word of praise for a job well done. With still another, it may be an offer of help when the work is stacking up.

The appropriate touch, McGrath says, will become clear as the managerial relationship develops. But the point is that the manager must acknowledge these kinds of things as part of the job and not as some onerous task that is one more example of coddling people.

The final requirement of good managing in today's changed world, McGrath claims, is the ability to undo—to say "I'm sorry" when you have

Managers must serve the needs of workers

behaved badly to your people or when you have simply made a mistake.[2] Most people in positions of authority have believed that this would be a grave admission of weakness or of failure. Because of our belief that managers can't make mistakes or be wrong, this has practically become a taboo in the organization world. Yet it is really the beginning of building any sort of team spirit in an organization to acknowledge that the leadership is not infallible and that some of the talented people on the payroll just might be able to contribute to the solution of the organization's problems.

Those who have normally objected to managing people in the style McGrath advocates have based their skepticism on the belief that it would not work, that order and discipline would break down, and that the whole enterprise eventually would founder. They have been remarkably successful in resisting the recommendations of management consultants and organization psychologists who have been arguing the need for change.

It is ironic that one of the industrial heroes of the Japanese is an American efficiency expert, W. Edwards Deming, a man most American managers have never heard of. Today, Japanese productivity and Japanese competition in international markets may dilute some of our traditional resistance to changing the way we manage people. Again, one of the ironies in this situation is that the Japanese listened to the American experts we dismissed as woolly thinkers.

In the late 1950s and early 1960s one of the leading electronics firms in the Southwest did some landmark studies on employee participation in their work—in its design and execution. One finding of the studies was that workers had a primary set of needs having to be satisfied before there was any hope of winning their enthusiastic support.

The first was simple mastery of the job, to get to the point at which they could feel that they could do the job comfortably and competently.

After achieving a sense of mastery, workers then needed to have a predictable work environment. They wanted to know the probable consequences of any given action. If they were late, what happened? If they made a mistake, what happened? If they did a good job, what happened?

Once they had job mastery and predictability of the work environment, workers needed to be valued as people. They were developing an attachment to the organization and wanted reciprocal treatment. Put simply, they wanted to be loved. (As an aside, it is generally acknowledged in the United States that one of the secrets of the great worker loyalty engendered by the Japanese is their policy of practically guaranteeing their workers a job for life. In contrast, most American workers live with the gnawing belief that they are expendable and will be let go when the organization falls on bad times.)

Once people in this southwestern company had job mastery, predictability in the work environment, and a sense that they were valued, they were ready to give something of themselves back. It was at this point that they felt a sense of ownership of the job and were ready to give their productivity and loyalty. Without that foundation, the researchers concluded, there was no sense in threatening, exhorting, or pleading for productivity and participation, for they simply would not be forthcoming.

Clearly, Father McGrath is on sound human behavioral ground when he argues that in today's world we cannot rely on automatic values which are no longer automatic. Authority, loyalty, and discipline are crucial organizational values for any successful enterprise, but they cannot be mandated. They must be earned through managing people on the basis of good human relationship.

When these values are earned, then authority takes its legitimacy not from fear but from respect and concern. Loyalty, in similar fashion, is not the blind variety; it is a loyalty of mutual concern, mutual trust, and caring. And discipline will not be external discipline based on rules and regulations and sanctions. It will be self-discipline of people working for common goals that they understand and share and for which they are willing to pay some sort of pain price—for example, their own individual short-term desires.

So we come back to the questions posed at the beginning of this chapter. What does the work force want in terms of better communication? What must management be prepared to do—and how? And what should be the priorities for more effective worker communication?

The first question is relatively easy to answer. The work force wants to know the organization's prospects for success and the issues which jeopardize that success. Further, they want all this expressed in terms that mean something to them. They also want a human presence in the form of a boss to whom they can relate, a boss who knows what's going on and who accepts it as part of his or her job to share information and to be an intermediary to and from the organization.

What management must be prepared to do is easier to say than to do. It must be prepared to share information consistently, accurately, and truthfully through its formal media and through its managers. Once again, by "information" I don't mean every little bit of unrelated data that can be gathered and dumped on people. I mean information that has been shaped into clear issues which can be communicated in terms of significance to anyone who has a perceived stake in the organization's well-being.

That, in turn, requires a planned and well managed effort. It also requires the organizational will to make the sharing of information a top priority, rating senior management time and support and the frank acknowledgment that people have a right to such information.

In my mind, there are two primary priorities. The first is developing an understanding of the issues in and around the organization and finding out how they can be communicated systematically to the organization's employees and other audiences. The second is finding out how to energize the typical line manager to understand his or her communication role and to perform it. Again, that role is easier to identify than to perform, because in practice we have not made those kinds of demands on managers, who had only to meet their objectives and stay under budget to be successful. Now we will be asking a great deal more.

Management consultant Scott Myers tells a story that shows at once how simple and complex this communication task is. He was called in by a client to suggest how the management might communicate better with its work force. It seems that the company was a traditional organization which was trying to update itself and its practices. In his initial discussion with the president, Myers was told that some preliminary work had already been done and that the company was about to spend several hundred thousand dollars to install closed-circuit television equipment throughout the premises so that messages could be transmitted quickly to all employees.

Myers was dismayed by this solution to the problem and asked that the order be delayed for a short time until he could size up the situation and make some suggestions. The president agreed reluctantly and sat down with Myers to review with him the history of their communication efforts. In the course of doing that, Myers discovered a quaint but interesting practice at the company. For some years, the employees shared a common coffee break during which all the company's coffee machines were programmed to dispense free coffee. At the same time a pastry cart was wheeled into each area with free pastries for everyone.

Myers watched the proceedings one morning with interest and recognized an opportunity. At his next meeting with the president, he suggested that the president have coffee with his people out in the corridor where the pastry carts were set up. The president smiled patiently and said that he couldn't do that. When Myers asked why not, the president's reply was the classic one: it simply wasn't done. The executives of the company all had their coffee in their own offices from a special mahogany cart that was wheeled into their quarters. They never mingled with the company employees at coffee break time. It would have been bad form. It might even be seen as an intrusion.

Myers persisted, however, and reluctantly the president agreed to try having a cup of coffee with his people. The first attempt was an abysmal failure. The president didn't even know how to work the coffee machine. In fact, some bystander watching the man fumble with his coins to get a free cup of coffee finally had to walk over and assist him. Red faced, the executive took the cup in hand and looked for someone to begin a conversation with. Unfortunately, the employees were all clustered in their little groups quietly discussing their various concerns and glancing curiously at the president.

The executive drank his coffee and walked back to his office, where he pronounced the experiment a flop. Myers listened to the description of what had happened and said that the problem was twofold. One, the president had left his coat on, and he should have gone out there in his shirt-sleeves. Two, the employees just weren't used to seeing their president in their area. To make this a fair test, Myers said that the experiment had to be repeated tomorrow. It took a good deal of convincing, and at first the president was emphatic in his refusal to subject himself to such humiliation again, but eventually he agreed to try it one more time—without his coat.

This time he managed to get his coffee without incident and to break into the perimeter of one of the little groups. After some initial conversation about the weather, he even asked how things were going and got some pleasantries from the group, indicating that everything was fine. The next day he decided to do some homework about a current concern of the work force about parts delivery. Intentionally, he raised the subject with the group and asked them about what they thought might be done. He was surprised that he soon found himself in the middle of an animated conversation.

The next day and the next, he went out to the corridor for his morning coffee and discussion. In time he found himself holding forth on all kinds of company issues and concerns with his workers, who now felt comfortable enough to discuss their concerns. It was all working so successfully that he asked his senior staff also to begin mingling with their people at coffee time, and he soon canceled the television equipment in favor of the simpler and more effective technique of firsthand, face-to-face communication.[3]

What are the lessons? There are many. The first lesson is that the dramatic solutions are frequently not the best. Television would have done little or nothing to correct the problem at this company. In fact, it might have increased the distance between management and the workers. Television is an impressionistic medium, and, unfortunately, one of the impressions that it sometimes gives is that the era of Big Brother is coming, with all human communication reduced to electronic signals shown on television monitors.

The second lesson is that status and trappings get in the way of good organizational communication. People are awed and intimidated by power, and so much of what goes on in organizations tends to emphasize that power and status difference. Why is it that senior management always occupy the top floors of their buildings? Why do they always have the largest and fanciest offices? Why do they have reserved parking places? Why do they go in for private executive dining rooms?

The usual answer is that members of senior management have worked hard to get to the positions they now occupy, and they deserve these things as their just rewards. That may be true, but status and power also represent a cost to the organization. They are barriers to good communication and tend to promote a daily acting out of the tale of the emperor's new clothes. None of the subjects, except one or two bold ones, has the courage to tell him that he is naked.

Consultant David Berlo claims that a hierarchical authority structure is about the worst kind of organization in which to move truth up and down. He asserts that lying and covering up are on the increase in contemporary organizations because mistakes are not allowed and because senior management is increasingly isolated by status and by its insistence on the trappings of power.

It's an interesting and, I think, valid argument. What person will press his or her luck by differing with the boss in the boss' opulent office? All the sensory signals around that conversation make it clear who is smarter, richer, and more powerful. Faced with opposition or intense questioning, the employee usually will back down and decide not to tell the boss what he or she may need to know to make a proper decision.

It is doubtful that hierarchy and status will be done away with, because they are too much a part of our organizational traditions, but we certainly have to find a way to overcome or work around them if we are to have any hope of carrying on effective communication between organizational leaders and the people they are trying to lead. A device as simple as mingling with workers during their coffee time may be the answer.

At least one Xerox senior manager I know holds what he calls "home court" meetings, where he leaves his own office and schedules meetings in the offices of the people in his function. Several others take every opportunity they can to meet with their people in informal groups for give-and-take discussions. Whatever the technique, senior managers badly need to find ways to reduce the barriers and isolation we have mutually perpetuated.

The third lesson we can draw from the coffee break story Myers tells is the surprising reluctance of senior managers to mingle with their people. In some few cases that is outright arrogance, but in the majority I suspect that it is shyness. In the past we have selected the best individual contributors and the cleverest politicians for our leadership. Rarely did anyone pay much attention to their "people skills." This is a deficiency we will have to correct in our selection criteria for future senior managers. Today's organizational world is simply too complex to ignore the communication skills (and comfort) of people who will be in leadership positions. The building of consensus and the communication of organizational priorities and vision are going to be the key to success in an industrial world that will inevitably become even more bewildering than it is today.

At this writing, there are only a relative handful of American corporations that are systematically and consistently trying to deal with the problems I describe in this book. And most of these are doing it at a level of sophistication and commitment that, to put it kindly, leaves a lot to be desired. The majority merely attempt to fill their communication gaps with printer's ink. A few have ventured into electronic communication with very mixed results, and only a dozen or so are systematically looking at ways to take advantage of the manager as communicator.

There is increasing emphasis in the communication profession on the need for institutional organizations to identify issues and communicate their positions, but even that aspect of organizational communication remains rudimentary in practice. The point is that there is both the need and opportunity to do much better than we have. But for this to happen, institutional leadership must define the problem and muster the will to deal with it.

I said earlier that the nay-sayers have been remarkably successful in keeping this from happening. These opponents argue that there is no real need to do this sort of communicating with the work force, that employees are apathetic about the organization, that all employees want is a job and to be left alone, and that there certainly is no obligation for a private concern to share its plans and strategies. To a senior management that is terribly aware of the real risks inherent in good communication those are apparently compelling arguments. That they also happen to be fallacious hasn't made a whole lot of difference in organizational practice.

The responsibility for communication leadership—and indeed the ownership of the communication process and problem—rests with senior management. It is always a disaster when they try to delegate by hiring a sort of tribal medicine man to do the communicating in their stead. What is required is that they actively address the process with the help of competent professionals. That's no more and no less than any other major organizational activity gets or deserves.

The balance of this book will show why and how communication must be managed properly for the sake of corporate truth.

NOTES

1. Thomas A. McGrath, S.J., "The Changing Role of a Manager," an address to the 1979 Annual Seminar of the Industrial Communication Council, New Orleans, October 1979.
2. Ibid.
3. Scott Myers, "Supporting, Training, and Encouraging Managers as Communicators," an address to the 1979 Annual Seminar of the Industrial Communication Council, New Orleans, October 1979.

Chapter 3

Management IS Communication

In our various institutional organizations we are confused and ambivalent as well as a bit weary when we reflect on the manager's responsibility to communicate. On the one hand, we have sermonized to managers so much about the need for better communication that practically everyone believes that improved communication would be a good thing. On the other, we have been unclear about when managers should talk and when they should keep their mouths shut.

While repeating our various pieties about the need for better communication, we have also saddled managers with a long list of priority responsibilities that they must attend to. At the top of the list has been the need to attain bottom line financial numbers almost regardless of how they do it. In fact, it has been clear to most managers in practically any organization we can think of that they need do two things to survive. First, they must attain the various objectives they have contracted for in their business plan. Second, they must not overspend their budgets in doing so. Success has generally been gauged by those two measurements.

In recent years, however, we have added some other demands. We have said that it is important to manage the organization's human resources carefully and thoughtfully. (In this regard we have said that managers must not discriminate, play favorites, tyrannize, sexually harass, invade the privacy of, threaten, or otherwise abuse the people entrusted to their care.) The trouble is, in most cases, we have not made all this a measurable or rewardable part of the managerial job; so most managers have not taken these responsibilities as seriously as the two primary ones of meeting objectives and being financially prudent.

If we accept the truism that managing means getting work done through other people, then managers early in their careers need to come to grips with how this job can be done. Most beginning managers believe that there are only two options. They can be autocratic and order people to do the work—or else. Or they can persuade and cajole and appeal to the self-interest of the work force. The first way could be characterized roughly as the traditional approach; the second might be termed the contemporary approach. There are lots of variations on those two themes, but they are the two major ones in our various institutions.

As McGregor and other management thinkers have reminded us, each of these two options has its roots in our view of human nature. If we see humankind as essentially lazy, sinful, and badly in need of direction and supervision, we will tend to be more autocratic and to rely on what Father McGrath has called the once-automatic values of authority, loyalty, and discipline.

If we see humankind more optimistically—essentially anxious to contribute, to make a difference, and to be responsive to the trust we put in them as well as to be motivated by appeals to their self-interest—we will tend to be more willing to explain and share responsibility.

The Japanese have a charming folktale they use to describe the difference between their management approach and ours in the United States. They tell of the time that the sun and the wind decided to have a contest to see who could get a man to remove his coat first. The wind blew fiercely at the man in an effort to rip his coat from his body with ferocious gusts of cold air. The harder the wind blew, the more tenaciously the man clung to his coat, and eventually the wind gave up.

The sun smiled at the wind's folly and began gently and almost caressingly to raise the temperature around the man. As it got warmer and warmer, the man did the logical thing: he removed his coat to make himself more comfortable.

The American approach to human resource management, say the Japanese, is more like the tactics of the wind. It emphasizes rugged individualism, rationalism, and risk taking. The Japanese system emphasizes paternalism, decision making based on consensus, and careful planning and testing.

In practice, most American managers today would get poor marks on their skill or willingness to communicate—despite all the emphasis we have put on management training and development in recent years. Why should this be so? Managers should want to do better in this vital area, one would think.

A clue to what is wrong can be found in another of our fictional companies —XYZ Associates, a fast-growing computer company in the time-sharing business. XYZ is headquartered in San Diego and employs 9000 people across the United States. The company's annual sales are $150 million, and in its relatively brief history it has grown at an almost explosive rate.

The growth has been a mixed blessing, since XYZ has had to do very quickly what other companies are able to accomplish in a generation or two of maturation. People who were primarily successful entrepreneurs two or three years ago have had to become successful corporate bureaucrats who could manage growth and change while building an organization. In several cases, they simply could not handle their new job responsibilities, and XYZ has had to recruit more-seasoned managers from other corporate organizations. This action has created sizable morale problems, since XYZ people who were around from the earliest days see their career opportunities dwindling and their careers dead-ended.

At this writing Dave Otter, XYZ president and founder, is deeply disturbed with the findings of a study by an independent consultant engaged to tell him why his managers don't seem to be communicating effectively with their people. Otter's human resources vice-president, Kevin O'Flynn, persuaded him to do the study to determine how communication could be improved at XYZ. O'Flynn's original interest was triggered by a finding by one of his staff people that the communication items on XYZ's standard attitude survey were a predictor of the overall attitude survey findings. Quite simply, if the communication items were favorable, the survey was going to turn out favorably. If they were negative, the survey itself would be negative. Intrigued by these findings, the vice-president hired a consulting firm to tell him more.

As O'Flynn reflected on the problem with his staff, he began to believe that managers at XYZ didn't communicate for one of two basic reasons.

O'Flynn's first guess was that it was a skills problem. The managers hadn't been trained in the niceties of effective communication and were not comfortable with it. Therefore, they hesitated to expose their shortcomings to their people. If this was so, then it was clear that the fairly simple solution was a good communication training program for managers.

O'Flynn's second guess was that the problem stemmed from XYZ managers themselves not always being sure of what was going on. The company moved so fast that it was difficult for the managers to know at any given time what was actually happening to the business. Faced with a dearth of information, O'Flynn reasoned, the managers simply avoided the embarrassing questions they suspected their people would pose in a staff meeting or similar forum. If this were the case, then the solution was to provide a good information program for managers.

XYZ's consultant designed a study the consulting firm proposed to conduct in several typical XYZ units. The plan was to interview the unit's senior manager, his or her staff, and then first-line supervisors as well as typical working-level people. All the interviews were to be one-on-one sessions with fairly open-ended opportunities to provide answers.

The results caught O'Flynn by surprise, since XYZ managers said that from their perspective there were two major problems. The first was that nowhere in their job experience had it been made clear to them that communication was a major XYZ priority. The managers knew that they were paid for meeting the numbers they were assigned each month. That was the job, not communicating with people. If your numbers were good, your reviews were good, and you were rewarded. If your numbers were bad, your reviews equally were bad, and you were penalized.

This finding is a classic case of a not-well-enough-understood fact: organizations speak at least three languages to their people. The first is the language of words, a fact most of us understand very well. The second, however, is the language of actions, and this is a brand of communication that all too often we overlook. Third, organizations also speak to people in their policies, and this certainly is a language we hardly ever notice. XYZ policy had clearly communicated the priorities to XYZ managers.

The second major problem alarmed O'Flynn even more than the first. XYZ managers acknowledged in the survey that despite their compulsion to chase numbers and have little time for anything else, they were not stupid and knew from their Harvard MBA work and XYZ management courses that communication is a vital tool for getting things done. In essence, they promised the interviewers that if they could ever get any relief from the numbers race they would communicate better and more often with their people. "But for now," they said, "we just don't have the time."

Those words stuck in O'Flynn's craw, because it was a clear indication of one of the great fallacies American management lives by: the belief that communication is a separate, somehow extracurricular activity to be engaged in when all the meetings are over, all the paperwork is done, and all the phone calls are returned. O'Flynn knew that communication is not separate from managing. It *is* managing. Or, better said, management is communication.

This insight is crucial to the task of consistent and well managed communication. Indeed, if we are convinced of that, there is no choice about good organizational communication. If we are to manage our people well, we must communicate well. The two are the same task. That's the good news.

The bad news is that if we neglect good management communication practices, as most companies have tended to do, we put the whole operation in jeopardy. If that's true, the devil's advocates among us may ask, then how is it that there are so many seemingly successful corporate enterprises? The answer is that many of these enterprises have not been tested in the fires of intense competition or corporate adversity. When they are, they'd better have their communication strategy carefully developed and properly managed, or they will be in for serious trouble.

When XYZ got to the employee level in its survey, it found a wide range of communication complaints. People said that they were rarely told why things were done. They were simply told that "it was policy" or that "some bird at corporate headquarters" took it in mind to issue the new directive or change the procedure.

They also complained that no one listened to their suggestions or their ideas for doing the job better. Two things tended to happen. Either there was no response to a suggestion—or the boss stole the idea and took credit for it. In both cases the people reported that they were discouraged by the reaction and stopped making suggestions because they clearly weren't welcome at XYZ.

They also complained that there was no upward channel of communication.

When reminded of XYZ's open-door policy, whereby any employee could take a complaint to any level of the organization, they laughed and said that they believed that to do such a thing would be suicidal. The employees said that even if they didn't get you directly, there were subtle things they could do to make life miserable. As several XYZ people put it, "I would only use the open-door policy if I were desperate or if I didn't care what happened to me."

Managers complained further that they really had no idea of what sort of communication role XYZ expected them to play. As one put it, "All they ever say is that it's good to communicate. What does that mean? What do they want me to do? Hold more meetings? Listen to people? I don't know what the hell they're talking about, and I don't think they do either."

The XYZ story is typical of the situation at most large and small North American companies. The key question is "What can we and should we do about it?" One of the best answers I know is embodied in a model we developed at Xerox of a manager's communication responsibility. That model attempted to define expectations and to give the manager some notion of what good management communication involved.[1]

The model begins with the assertion that one of the most basic tasks of management is to tell people what the job is and how they are doing. This is a responsibility to the entire group of people being managed, and it is meant to be done on a group basis rather than one-on-one. It means that the manager sits down with his or her people and tells them at appropriate intervals what group goals are and how and why they might be changing. It means that he or she also keeps the group informed of how they are doing as a team. Figure 3.1 shows some of the basic subjects that the manager must cover with the entire work group assembled together in one meeting.

Obviously, this first task is not something that would need to be done weekly. But it must be attended to at reasonably frequent intervals if people are to understand that they are indeed part of an overall effort which must be merged with the efforts of other work groups for the sake of the overall effectiveness of the organization.

The second part of the manager's communication responsibility, as we defined it at Xerox, is to be certain that people understand their own individual jobs and the standards for success on those jobs. This part tells the manager to discuss job responsibility appropriately, naturally, and routinely with each individual on a one-to-one basis. The major issue to be addressed here is what is expected of the individual in his or her job, together with the standards against which he or she will be measured. This is the area that is so often neglected in the work place, since we assume that people know what they are doing and why merely because they look busy or seem proficient. This is also the area in which the manager is urged to gather and pay attention to the subordinate's job suggestions and to questions about the job itself or policies and procedures that can affect the job. In far too many cases at work, these issues are taken for granted, ignored, or somehow deemed unnecessary to be discussed. The result is that the

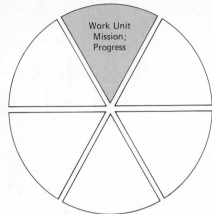

Discuss:

- Work unit's mission

- Work unit's objectives, targets

- Accomplishments of the work unit

- Subordinates' questions and suggestions on mission/progress

Figure 3.1   Work Unit Mission; Progress

average worker is left to learn the job from his or her coworkers and in the process to pick up their work habits, both good and bad. The major issues to be addressed in this part of the communication model are listed in Figure 3.2.

The third part of the manager's communication responsibility is the traditional one of giving people performance feedback. No communication responsibility is more important than this one for the simple reason that people need to know how well they are doing if they are to have any hope of doing a better job. The most common vehicle for expressing this feedback in industry is the performance appraisal, that once-a-year session when the boss and his or her subordinate sit down to talk about the year's work. In far too many cases, the session is a travesty.

At one extreme, all the worker's errors and shortcomings are swept under

Figure 3.2   Individual Job Responsibility Standards

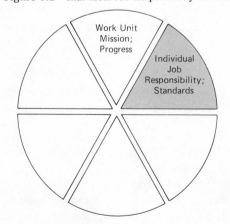

Discuss:

- Subordinate's job responsibility, standards

- Subordinate's job suggestions

- Questions about the job

- Policies and procedures affecting job

the corporate rug, and the worker is led to believe that there is no imaginable way the job could be done better. In such cases the manager simply doesn't have the courage to deal with performance problems and takes the easy way out. He or she finds no fault.

The other extreme is to focus so pointedly and so exclusively on shortcomings that the worker hears nothing positive in the appraisal discussion. In too many organizations, the only time people get any performance feedback is during the once-a-year review. The rest of the time there is relative silence unless they make a serious mistake.

Or all too often, the performance appraisal is a carefully planned ambush at which the manager unloads all his or her frustrations about the subordinate's work habits and personality traits. The end result of such a session is a demoralized employee who really believes he or she is in deep trouble.

Granted that performance interviews are often strained and mismanaged, what can be done to improve the process? One answer is to be sure that such reviews are done frequently instead of once a year. That way this kind of discussion is a normal occurrence and not a mandatory annual discussion. Under these circumstances, both parties will be more comfortable and less defensive. Another requirement is to be certain that the person being reviewed is praised and recognized for good performance. As a rule, managers are more accustomed to finding fault than they are to saying "thank you." The problem, I believe, is this: managers have been conditioned to believe that if they express too much appreciation they will be hit up for a raise or a promotion. So they believe it is better to behave simply as though "that's what you're paid for around here." As Father McGrath and others remind us, it is crucial for managers to say the right words to their people to foster and build appropriate human relationships. This means caring enough to praise and caring enough to criticize. Figure 3.3 suggests some major points that need to be covered in effective performance feedback. Note that the emphasis is on a dialogue that is held with some regularity and focuses on what we can do together to make the individual more effective on the job.

Figure 3.4 focuses on perhaps the most important part of the model in today's North American corporate culture. It is the most important because it is traditionally the one we have been most inclined to ignore. Every individual brings to the job a unique bundle of pluses and minuses, strengths and vulnerabilities, worries and concerns. The tradition in most organizations has been to say to people that all that must be left at the gate when they come to work. There is no place for feelings that interfere with the work.

The end result all too often is that people in emotional turmoil have found few sympathetic shoulders on bosses. A divorce, the death of a spouse or child, and other grave upsets might elicit an outpouring of sympathy initially, but it was clear that "you have to put this behind you and get back to your work." Less traumatic problems that affect all of us and sometimes alter performance got practically no sympathy until recent years. Hence the working mother was expected to leave her sick children with the baby-sitter, travel schedules were to be

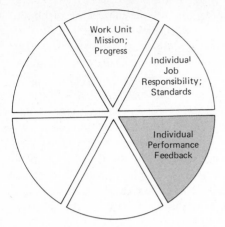

Communicate:

- Performance appraisal fully and on time

- Personal appreciation for effective performance

- Areas for performance improvement, as needed

- With subordinate about actions to improve performance, as needed

- Individual's value to work unit

Figure 3.3   Individual Performance Feedback

met regardless of the inconvenience to families or worker, and the transfer to another city was expected to be accepted with a click of the heels and a resigned call to the moving company. The old slogan we all know too well applied almost without exception: "If you don't like it here, go someplace else."

Although a lot of this still lingers on in too many institutional organizations, things have improved noticeably. A mark of that improvement is the emerging belief that an important managerial role is listening, referral, and counseling. This is an area ripe for individual experimentation and creativity because, until recently, we have not seen it as a significant part of a manager's job. Figure 3.4 shows some of the more obvious possibilities. The point is a simple one. A good manager must be prepared to deal with the individual as a person; he or she must care about the individual and express that care appropriately.

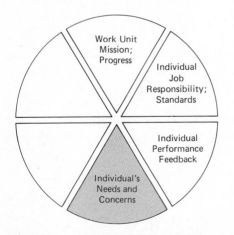

Communicate:

- Willingness to listen to personal concerns

- Timely feedback by manager to all job-related concerns, suggestions, questions

- Willingness to listen impartially to discrimination complaints

- Willingness to listen to employee relations problems

- Opportunities for career advancement

- Your need for feedback regarding your performance as a manager

- Willingness to assist subordinates in resolving their conflicts

Figure 3.4   Individual's Needs and Concerns

The next part of the model is an area ripe for the harnessing of human creativity and imagination. It is no secret that the people in the best position to improve job performance are the people who actually must do the work. If they know the job, if they understand the work environment and its unique culture, and if it is clear to them that such suggestions will be received gratefully and acted upon, when possible, there is an excellent chance that the workers will engage in clever and intelligent problem solving on the job. The success of the Japanese and several American companies with quality circles is a perfect example of this principle. In the quality circle a group of concerned and caring workers do their best to pool their ideas for doing the job better. But that doesn't happen unless it is clear that the boss is receptive. The boss is the pivotal person in carrying suggestions and proposals from his or her people to the right decision maker for action. The major types of this kind of upward communication are shown in the next diagram, Figure 3.5.

Finally, the people in a work unit need to understand that what they are doing as a group somehow makes a difference. The service team or accounting unit or maintenance crew all need to understand that their work affects and supports others and that it's important to the whole. Figure 3.6 identifies the major tasks to be performed by the manager in helping people understand the work unit's place in the organization.

Looking at all the parts of the model together, it's clear that communication is the lifeblood of the management process. Figure 3.7 shows why. Parts 1–3 of the model provide people with the opportunity for job mastery and a predictable work environment. These three parts equate roughly with the popular management by objectives technique. Part 4 is people's need to be appreciated, to be approved, and even to be loved. Normally, we prefer the lower-voltage concept we call "recognition," but it undeniably is an ingredient in managing and leading any group of people.

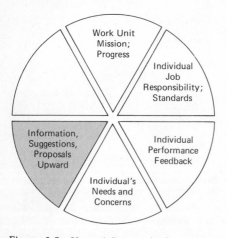

Communicate upward:

- Successes and failures of the work group in meeting objectives

- Problems in, or obstacles to, meeting objectives

- Suggestions for senior management actions, policy changes

- Proposals to address opportunities, efficiencies

Figure 3.5   Upward Communication

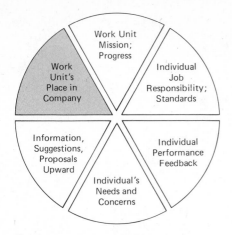

Discuss:

- How the work unit's mission affects the whole

- Major business issues affecting the work unit

- Basic business strategy of the work unit

- Role of other work units, as needed

- All business actions (e.g., reorganizations, RIF, etc.) affecting work unit

Figure 3.6   Work Unit's Place in Company

THE MANAGER'S COMMUNICATION RESPONSIBILITY

(Two-Way Communication on Each of These Six Major Tasks)

Figure 3.7   The Manager's Communication Responsibility

Join those four parts and what they are likely to produce is a turned-on, committed, caring worker. Add the next two parts that further define the work environment. Then offer the opportunity to influence that environment (parts 5 and 6), and it is a good bet that people can and will be more productive.

If all this is true, then why don't managers simply behave like this and make productivity problems go away? Aside from the productivity problem having a variety of complex and not-terribly-well-understood causes in addition to this one of poor human resource management, the solution is not that easy. The brief explanation can be found in the culture of so many organizations that, like our fictional XYZ Associates, do not recognize, reward, or reinforce such managerial behavior.

Let's invent and look at a different kind of institutional organization than XYZ. This one we'll call Miracle Bakeries. Miracle is one of the last of the old-time bakeries that delivers to homes in upstate New York. The route salespeople all drive large vans along the rural customer routes they have built up over the years. Once a large enterprise in terms of people and trucks on the road, Miracle has been hit hard by the cost of energy and inflating payroll costs. It is more and more difficult to justify its home delivery service, and there is considerable management sentiment to abandon it.

The typical Miracle driver-salesperson is an interesting study. He (and in the last 10 years or so she) enjoys providing an unusual customer service in today's impersonal consumer age. The Miracle driver traditionally has been a welcome figure selling bread, desserts, potato chips, and similar products from house to house. In the middle of a long and rushed day, most drivers still find time to sit down for a cup of coffee in an isolated farmhouse or to make conversation with a lonely urban housewife hemmed in by bad winter weather. In fact, the real satisfaction of working at Miracle has never been the marginal salary and benefits but the customer contact.

As sales have declined and the large city bakery has given way to regional baking centers, where products are produced on an automated, almost-assembly-line basis, the drivers have become increasingly apprehensive about the future—and for good reason. A recent report from a Miracle consultant suggests a radical redesign of the delivery system to the customer. The consultant's proposal says that Miracle's only hope for survival is to become more cost effective, to stop giving the same service to every customer irrespective of sales potential, to eliminate all rural delivery routes because of the cost of fuel, and to consolidate city routes for the most efficient driving patterns. The consultant has also proposed that a computer be used to program the day's deliveries, with customers calling their orders in the day before. In this way she hopes to reduce the endless discussions in customer kitchens as children linger over family selections from the driver's delivery basket.

For commercial accounts, she has proposed a radio dispatch system so that drivers can be directed to them as supplies run low. This last recommendation really rankled the drivers because most of them did not enjoy working the commercial accounts anyway. The drivers protested that the volume was not good enough because the stores saw them as a home delivery service and because so many stores now baked their own bread and pastries.

As the suggestions are implemented one by one, the drivers have become more and more distressed. In a job in which customer relationships are the main psychic income, the loss of these relationships is demoralizing. There are threats of work slowdowns, rumors of unionization, and even some small evidence of sabotage of the radio dispatch system. Miracle management is increasingly alarmed. The 10 sales supervisors are feeling the brunt of the discontent and are handling the hostility in a classic manner. "Look," they plead, "they're making me do this. You know me. If it were up to me, nothing would change. I'm just following orders."

At a meeting of the sales supervisors, Fred Kowalsky, president of Miracle, explodes at the resistance to the changes. He reminds all the supervisors that the future of the company is riding on the success of this effort and that they had better bring their people into line. He tells them that they should want to make this system work, that it is in everyone's best interest to explain its benefits clearly. He closes the meeting by frankly admitting that he is confused and upset over the lack of cooperation after he had personally run the company with concern for Miracle people and as one big family.

When the supervisors gathered in a small group in the parking lot after the meeting, one of them expressed the view of the majority when he complained, "I don't get paid for that! Let Kowalsky go explain his own system if he thinks it's so important. I'm sick of the flak for something I had nothing to do with."

The reactions to the meeting of two of the supervisors are instructive. One took it all seriously and called meetings of his route people on two successive mornings to discuss the changes. Unfortunately, he missed his quota that week and explained the shortfall on the grounds that he had taken the drivers off the road to talk. His supervisor snapped at his excuse, saying, "Your job is not to hold meetings. It's to sell our products, and you don't do that in the shop asking a lot of questions no one can answer."

A second supervisor decided to apply the heat. He threatened his drivers, saying that he would check their every move, that he was sick of the moaning and groaning, and that anyone who didn't meet quota would answer to him. He hinted darkly of a reapportioning of routes. The result was that everyone went out and sold at a pace they clearly could not sustain much beyond a week or two. But the sales supervisor was named supervisor of the month with his picture displayed in the main lobby at Miracle!

In two years Miracle was out of the home delivery business and had fired most of its drivers, trying to make a go of it as one more commercial bakery.

The Miracle case is instructive for many reasons. An organization caught up in painful change that required everyone to perform his or her job in a new and not necessarily agreeable way, Miracle was not prepared to deal with change or to help its people understand the necessity for it. When its management did begin to deal with the necessary changes, it did so at the eleventh hour and with the mistaken notion that everyone would understand this need and respond uncomplainingly because so much was at stake. The final blow came when nothing was done in the organization to reinforce the need, the message, or the manager who was supposed to deliver the message.

This scenario is typical of such cases. People somehow believe that the process will simply take care of itself. Management will sound the alarm, and the faithful will respond. At Miracle, management initially sent no signals to the work force about their plans. Then they sent signals of impending panic and disaster. And, finally, they mixed the signals by penalizing the behavior they should have been reinforcing and by reinforcing supervisory behavior that had little to do with their long-term problems. It's not surprising that Miracle wound up with a confused work force that felt little identification with the company's problems, much less any feeling of ownership of those problems.

How should the situation have been handled? Kowalsky and his staff should have foreseen that the changes they were instituting would be upsetting. They should have shared their plans as early as they could with their supervisors. They should have acquainted the supervisors with the circumstances that were influencing these changes, and they should have worked for their understanding and commitment.

In the process they undoubtedly would have faced some hostility and resistance, but there would have been the opportunity for the supervisors to ventilate those feelings. Once that was done, they, in all likelihood, would have stated the case as well as they could to their people—with a sense of ownership.

Then the supervisor's efforts could and should have been reinforced by senior management in employee meetings and whatever communication vehicles Miracle had in place or could invent for the occasion. And, of course, there should have been the expressed willingness to change any of these programs and business strategies as necessary if any of them were unworkable or unproductive.

The difference in the two approaches is the difference between trying to manage through authority and the presumed automatic responses of loyalty and discipline and trying to manage by means of informed relationships. The difference is also in seeing employees as mere extensions of the organization who can be programmed autocratically to perform or in seeing them as intelligent and mature people who will respond to reason. The values, needs, expectations, and capabilities of today's work force are much more compatible with the latter approach.

David Berlo, who has observed and commented on organizational communication for some years, claims that in the last 30 years we have been in the throes of a second industrial revolution in the United States. He believes that power in organizations is no longer in the hands of the senior leadership of those organizations, that it really has been diffused throughout the organization, and that the persons in charge of the organization's *real* options often have little in the way of status or authority. These people merely control the response of the organization to events. The trick is to remove the barriers between these people and the leadership that is held accountable for the organization's success.

In developing his thesis, Berlo reminds us that before the industrial revolution led us to the relatively new condition of the concentration of resources and people in large bureaucratic organizations talk in the work place was largely a trivial matter. People *showed* one another their work and how to perform that work by apprenticing a learner to a master.

With the coming of large organizations, talk was no longer trivial. It became essential for such organizations to cultivate the art of communication. The trouble was that organizations cultivated communication mainly as a means for powerful institutional leaders to impose their will on others. Communication became a process of broadcasting orders from the leader to all his followers. This process translated the leader's authority into direction, into actions for other people to take.

Berlo asserts that the changing nature of work, the complexity of the tasks people are now called on to perform, and the sheer size of modern work organizations all make that kind of communication an anachronism.[2] Contemporary leaders in any institutional organization are struggling to determine what is happening inside and outside the organization that may affect their plans and progress.

These leaders' frustration stems from an inability to find, with any real degree of certainty, the information they seek. Berlo is right when he claims that concentrated power of the kind that leaders knew before World War II in our society is gone. Information is no longer merely a tool of authority. It has actually replaced authority as the way to control the organization. Managers manage in today's organizations by sharing information, not by withholding it.

Intelligent institutional leaders, rather than searching for the best ways to protect information and to withhold it from people lower down in the organization, must search for information control systems that give people the information they need to do their work as well as to reduce the anxiety they feel about their role in the organization. All too often both of these needs have been denied by people who saw information as a means of sustaining their power. My knowledge of something, they reasoned, makes me more powerful than those who don't know what I know.

The fallacy in this reasoning is that in the modern work organization, with its specialization and vast numbers, the person lower down on the organizational ladder often gets information on his computer terminal before the leadership gets it. Worse yet, because of the vagaries and complexities of the chain of command, he or she often finds it virtually impossible to get the information to the leadership on a timely basis. In some cases, by the time it's reported, the information is no longer even true.

Clearly, the task is to create an organizational culture and an information support system that encourages and rewards the sort of management-employee relationship we must have in today's work place. The key word here is *system*. No longer can we assume that managers will truly manage any more than we can assume that they will truly communicate without incentives, direction, and plans. The task is far too important to continue to leave it to chance.

At Xerox some important beginnings have been made in developing a structure and a format for good human resource management—that is, a structure and format for good human communication. At the foundation of the structure is a system that encourages and rewards effective communication: a set of communication guidelines defines the company's expectations of its managers. These are the communication ideals that Xerox is trying to achieve as a corporation. They are important because they help define the corporate commitment to good communication and because they fix the responsibility of each level of management. The guidelines follow:

- Responsibility for the success of the Xerox communication program is vested in all Xerox managers.
- Communication leadership in any Xerox organization is the responsibility of that organization's senior management.
- Each manager is responsible to his or her manager and to his or her people for communication of the information on the state of the business, the tasks and goals of the organization, and the progress of the organization's work.
- Each manager owes it to his or her employees to pass their concerns and questions upward and to press for timely and responsive answers, if answers are not immediately available.
- Each manager is responsible to his or her people for candid communication on the individual's performance and career aspirations and for resolving misunderstandings of Xerox policy and its application.
- Employee self-esteem, as well as the quality of work life, can only be protected through continuing interpersonal and intergroup communication between employees and their manager.
- It is the responsibility of the senior manager of each Xerox operating unit to maintain an appropriate employee communication media program for the organization.
- In their communications with their people, all managers have an obligation to be forthright and timely in discussing objectives, results, problems, difficulties, and opportunities.[3]

As important as such guidelines are in articulating needs and responsibilities, they are not enough to have much effect by themselves. Even when they are coupled with the communication model described earlier in this chapter, they merely define expectations. A manager may be instructed by such materials; he or she may even be inspired and use them as guidelines for on-the-job behavior, but they will not change much of anything unless they are part of the planning cycle and reward system. True priorities in any organization are certified as such when they show up in the planning cycle and reward system. Until then they are only nice ideas.

The obvious advantage of a deliberate human resource management system is that it removes human resource management from the chaotic, slapdash kind of activity it all too often is in most large organizations. With such a system expectations are defined, human resource plans are developed by management closest to the problems, and results are carefully monitored and rewarded. The necessary end product is an institutional support system that encourages and aids the individual manager in doing better as a manager. The vital lubricant for that process is good managerial communication.

My professional colleagues in the communication business may wonder what their role is in the development of this kind of process in their own organizations. Given the way so many companies are organized, with specialists arbitrarily separated into different departments, that's a reasonable question. Too often the communication people are in a different department from the human resource people. In the ensuing turf battles over who should rightfully influence the communication process, the organization itself is the loser.

For an instructive example of how this dilemma can be handled, let's take another look at the XYZ case study mentioned earlier in this chapter. At XYZ Kevin O'Flynn is the vice-president of human resources. What this means is that the traditional personnel activities at XYZ—hiring, training, compensation, organization planning and development, personnel research, and various personnel services—are under O'Flynn. The professional communication activities—public relations, advertising, community and government relations, shareholder communication, and employee communication—are combined into a public affairs department headed by a director of public affairs, Ray Whittington. Whittington reports directly to XYZ's president, Dave Otter, but he is the only one reporting to Otter who is not a vice-president.

The tradition at XYZ is one of some rivalry and turf jealousy between human resources and the employee communication section, which reports to public affairs. Because employees and internal company matters are normally the province of human resources, it is imperative that the employee communication staff work closely with the human resources staff, but in practice there has been little in the way of effective communication.

What changed all that was the hiring of Dick Schultz as the manager of employee communication. Schultz was fascinated by the work that O'Flynn was doing on the difficulties of face-to-face communication by XYZ managers. In his earliest days on the job he met with O'Flynn to find out what he was up to and how the communication staff might be involved. Predictably, O'Flynn was guarded and close-mouthed at that first meeting. It was very clear that O'Flynn believed Schultz should be worrying about the production of XYZ media and not probing into personnel programs having little or nothing to do with those media.

Fortunately, Schultz was a bit of a diplomat and managed in time to win O'Flynn's confidence. How he did so is instructive for anyone who reflects on the damage that turf battles do in his or her organization. O'Flynn's manager of management training was Barbara Palmiere. Schultz quickly made friends with

Palmiere and explained why he was so interested in the work she had been doing on poor management communication. Although it may strike some that Schultz's interest should have been crystal clear to anyone with half a brain, that clarity is rarely perceived in most companies. Turf jealousy is real, and people have to be persuaded that the interest is in the problem and not in taking away part of their responsibility through political intrigue.

In brief, staff specialists in trying to deal with any problem as pervasive as the communication problem is must be prepared to build careful alliances with other staff specialists who also have an interest in the problem. In the beginning Palmiere had kept the management communication problem and her study a well-kept secret. The motivation was simple. Palmiere wanted to do the work, develop a solution, and present that solution to her senior management as her exclusive work. She hoped that she would get a pat on the head for her brilliance —and maybe even a promotion or a salary increase. She had no desire to share the glory for solving a problem that had long plagued XYZ management and was known to be one of the pressing concerns.

But the deeper she got into the project, the more frustrated she became. Part of the problem was that her background was mainly training, yet it was clear the solution to the management communication problem went far beyond a simple training program. That meant Palmiere would have to enlist the help of Schultz to design management information programs. In addition, she would have to enlist the help of several personnel staff specialists to find ways to begin building a human resource management system and change the very corporate culture of XYZ. To do that, she clearly needed the support of the most senior people in XYZ. Without their cooperation, nothing could be done.

Palmiere's initial temptation to go it alone is all too typical among staff people who want to be noticed and commended for their creativity and ingenuity in the face of a tough problem. To share the problem with someone is to share the recognition later. The problem is that when people go it alone in large organizations, their work is ignored or even undermined as too disruptive to the rest of the organization staff specialists, who are indifferent, or threatened, or downright hostile. The infamous not-invented-here factor rears its ugly head, and people begin looking for the flaws that every new scheme inevitably has. They point out the disruption it will mean and alarm anyone who will listen with their predictions of disaster if such a program is implemented. Most new proposals are just too fragile and vulnerable to permit this kind of pawing and jabbing. The result is that the proposals die in somebody's in-basket.

The solution at XYZ finally came when Palmiere and Schultz began to pool their ideas and to develop a joint proposal for their two bosses. The final proposal was a product of discussions with every staff specialist at XYZ who had an interest in the subject of managerial communication. When O'Flynn and Whittington began evaluating the joint proposal, they found almost universal agreement about its need and suitability. The reason was simple. Everyone felt a sense of ownership; they had been consulted, and consensus had been built before the joint proposal was ever submitted. Further, the proposal sailed through the XYZ executive committee because there was staff consensus that it was the best strategy for dealing with the problem.

The lesson once again is a simple one. Good staff work is almost always a product of good politicking in which ownership is created so that all can take credit for the needed solution. People in positions of power usually are well aware of who the key players have been, and these people generally get their due recognition and credit for a good solution to a tough problem.

Unfortunately, this process takes time and patience to carry out, and too many staff people—especially professional communication staff people—don't understand that. They want instant results and instant solutions to long-standing problems. In my view, a good staff person is like a long-distance runner. He or she must pace the run and must take satisfaction in small victories. Who ever saw a wildly cheering stadium filled with fans to greet those who finish a cross-country race? Distance runners are always the people who stagger in varying degrees of exhaustion across an improvised finish line on the track surrounding the football field. Worse, their moment of triumph is always at halftime while most of the football crowd is out buying a hot dog or watching the band make a block M. That's the fate of cross-country runners and staff specialists, but it's okay, because both move their respective organizations closer to their goals.

In the next chapter we'll take a look at the other major priority besides energizing the manager as the organization's primary spokesman both to and from his people. I refer to the task of defining and communicating the major issues that the organization is grappling with and doing so in a fashion that could be reasonably described as proactive rather than reactive.

NOTES

1. "Human Resources Management: The Manager's Communication Responsibility," Xerox publication 610P13248, 1980.
2. David Berlo, "The Power Issue: Who Is in Charge?," an address to the 1978 Annual Seminar of the Industrial Communication Council, New York, October, 1978.
3. *Managing in Xerox: A Handbook for Xerox Managers*, May 1981, p. 22; and *You and Xerox* (Employee Handbook), 1980, p. 30.

Chapter 4

How to
Communicate the Issues

Writing in *Organizational Dynamics* consultant Jerry Harvey relates an anecdote that has become a classic. He recalls visiting his in-laws in a small Texas town. It was a hot Sunday afternoon, and someone suggested as the family sat languidly on the porch that they ought to drive to Abilene for dinner. Seemingly, everyone agreed that the idea was a fine one, even though a 50-mile drive had to be made each way and the family car had no air conditioning. The meal turned out to be a disappointment, and the drive home seemed almost endless.

Once safely home, a tired and hot family member said that she had gone to Abilene reluctantly and that she would have preferred to stay home. In a voice edged with tones of self-sacrifice, she said she made the trip for the others. They sat in irritated and bemused disbelief as first one and then another admitted that he or she had never wanted to get in that hot car in the first place. They had all gone because they thought the others wanted to, and no one had the courage to protest.[1]

Work organizations are forever taking trips to Abilene because no one has the courage to protest. In its own way perhaps Watergate is a classic example. No one, as far as the record shows, ever said, "Wait, this is stupid behavior for the executive branch of the U.S. government. Do we really want to get mixed up in something as tawdry as this?" Instead, everyone involved seemed to have spent all their time trying to figure out how to make it work.

To some degree, the whole communication profession has been on an extended trip to Abilene, with management in the driver's seat. No where is this truer than in communication with employees, although it also applies to a large extent with the organization's other constituencies. The trouble is that this communication has been an attempt to report selectively the events experienced by the organization. It is a process based on the model of the public journalist who merely reports the facts with little or no attempt to embellish them. The organizational communicator and his or her management have merely reacted to events inside and outside the organization. When the organization was not sophisticated or large enough to have a professional communication person or staff, management simply did its best to keep people informed of events. In a good many cases management took the position that the process would take care of itself somehow or that people should be told only on a "need-to-know basis" in doing their jobs.

When there were communication professionals, too often they aped the public media, producing slick published articles to communicate the texture and substance of the organization. Or they resorted to visual media in response to the argument that people can't read any more. All these pieces had (or have) in common this fact: they were reporting positions and responses in reaction to events. They represented the apologies for what went wrong, or they were the elaborated defenses for what a company or other institutional organization had or had not done.

With employees this kind of reactive communication has led to an assumption that all an institutional organization needed was a good media program so management could tell its side of the story. That's a telling phrase—"its side of the story"—clearly suggesting an adversary relationship and a defense of management actions.

The trip to Abilene in this case is that most of us—management and professional communicators alike—took the easier and more obvious path of communicating reactively in media that couldn't possibly keep up with events. And even if the media could, it would have made little difference, because it isn't events that need to be communicated. It's trends and issues that people need to understand. By and large, the events are simply there, happening practically before our very eyes, and all that is required is that they be put into some sort of perspective and explained to us. That they have happened is obvious. The question is what do they mean?

If American institutional organizations are going to deal with the loss of confidence and the mistrust that have been growing in recent years, they must begin to develop new insights into the process of organizational communication.

Survey data accumulated by Opinion Research Corporation (ORC) over the last 25 years show that most institutional managements don't understand the communication process. Or if they do understand it, they haven't taken the trouble to develop a consistent and well conceived strategy for dealing with it.

Writing in the *Harvard Business Review,* Michael Cooper and other ORC researchers have documented value changes among employees that have been incubating for two and a half decades. What they see are demands for self-expression and self-fulfillment. They say:

The changes reported here are ubiquitous, pervasive, and nontransient; any reversal is unlikely in the foreseeable future. The goal for management is to be aware of and prepared for new and surfacing employee needs, before it is forced to take reactive, ignorant, and resistive postures. . . .

. . . What is undeniably required . . . is that corporations recognize the new realities within which they must function. The crucial issues then become the degree to which management can successfully identify, anticipate, and address these changing values as they surface. . . . But, make no mistake about it, changing employee values are no myth. They will be the realities that companies must face in the 1980s.[2]

Cooper puts his finger on the key issue for effective organizational communication with the employee constituency. If management is going to address the communication needs of the employee audience, it can only understand those needs by understanding the values that shape them. Then it must identify and talk about the organizational issues that most closely match those needs. And, of course, in the process it must identify, define, and articulate those issues that are the product of management's own perspective from the top of the organization. But for successful communication to happen, such issues must be tempered with and couched in terms that are important to the employee audience.

Typically, organizational communication has worked in almost the opposite way. Following the model of the journalist, the reporter of news, the organizational communicator and his or her management have simply reacted to events as they happened. The predictable result has been communication anarchy.

To understand why communication anarchy has resulted, let's take a look at the journalistic communication process in practically any organization we can think of. As we see in Figure 4.1, it is a reactive process that is always triggered by an event either inside or outside the organization. Obviously, that event must be significant enough to make some difference to the people who observe it—at least enough difference so that they are inclined to report it to others. If the event does not make any particular difference, it merely becomes one more ripple on the organization pond. In that case the communication process tends to bog down from lack of interest.

On the other hand, if the event has some significance and it has been witnessed by one or more persons, these people will invariably begin the process of recounting it to their coworkers. This process is always initiated by the informal channels of the organization through the ever-present grapevine. Irrespective of the organization, the grapevine normally has considerable credibility. People sometimes resent having to get their information from such a source, but the fact is that they usually believe what they hear from it.

Why this is so is instructive. If you think about what we call the grapevine and its mode of operation, you'll observe that it is a highly personal me-

Figure 4.1   EVENT

dium. Messages from the grapevine are delivered by other human beings face-to-face—usually people whom we know and trust and with whom we have enough experience to judge how much we should filter the message or how much of it we should discount altogether. Very often, as grapevine sources recount the latest to us, they become animated, excited, pleased, angered. They show us a whole range of human emotion and reaction to the message. They speculate about what it means, and they guess about the motives of the people responsible for the event. All in all, regardless of its limitations, getting messages through the grapevine is a satisfactory human experience that most of us take some pleasure in. Figure 4.2 outlines how the process begins to unfold.

In Figure 4.3 we see what happens when the formal channels are brought into play either to confirm or deny the grapevine message. No matter how we may pretend otherwise, the role of the formal channels is practically always confirmation or denial of what everyone already knows. Certainly, the formal channels are more accurate, more detailed, and more responsible, but it is rare that they are giving people substantially new information. The reason is that the formal channels presumably operate at management's discretion. (I say "presumably" because the option to communicate or not communicate is more apparent than real.)

All too often when a given message is spreading on the grapevine like a brushfire out of control, management convenes sweaty-palmed meetings to debate whether the event should be acknowledged formally. It is almost as if the event's existence could be denied by ignoring it. I have even heard people who should know better argue that we should say nothing because maybe nobody has noticed and our formal statement will merely dignify the event or confirm it. I must admit I don't hear that argument much anymore, but it was once used as the justification for keeping the formal channels silent. In the meantime, of course, the grapevine has broadcast the event everywhere with little or no regard for accuracy, personal reputations, or the dignity of those in control.

When those in charge of the formal channels do decide to recount a given

Figure 4.2

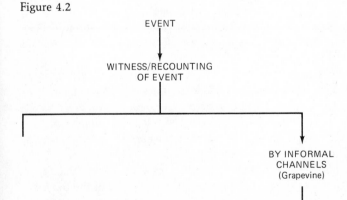

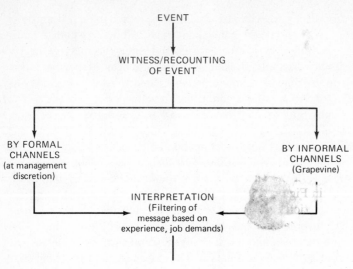

Figure 4.3

event through those channels, as we also see in Figure 4.3, the audience is left to interpret what they are hearing. The natural way the audience interprets the message is to filter it, generally on the basis of their experience with the other languages the organization speaks—namely, action and policy—as well as the job demands that are made on them as employees. It is, for example, difficult for someone in a department that spends lavishly on travel and the entertainment of customers to believe the message that the company is in a cost squeeze.

In interpreting the message he or she is receiving from both the grapevine and formal channels, the employee frequently tends to believe the grapevine and to be skeptical about the formal channels. Why this is so, I believe, has much to do with the method of delivery and the tone of the message. The method of delivery used by the grapevine is highly personal, almost intimate. The message is informal and frequently almost irreverent in its tone. It is one member of the organization talking frankly to another. In the best case, it is honest and reasonably charitable. In the worst case, it is deeply suspicious, cynical, and perhaps vicious.

The formal channels, on the other hand, usually dispense carefully laundered messages with each word measured and sometimes even slightly obscured to disguise an unpleasant reality or to put a better face on a particular action. It is not necessarily dishonest communication, but too often it is communication heavily laced with human ego. Careers and reputations are on the line in some of these communications, and everyone knows it.

Lest we be too harsh on those who shape the formal messages, it is important to remember that they are only doing what all of us do all of the time. We search for the best motives to explain our actions, minimize our responsibility for failures, and present our actions in the most favorable light we can think of.

The grapevine presents a nice balance to this human penchant for self-protection.

The other problem with this formal presentation of the event is that it is too formal. The language sounds like a parent talking to a child. It is stuffy. It is autocratic, and it is intended to gain the proper respect for the source of the message. The trouble is that it frequently has almost the opposite effect.

As we see in Figure 4.4, once the audience has properly filtered the message and compared the grapevine version with the formal version, the next step is speculation on causes and management motives. Why are "they" doing that? Who is at fault? What will they do about it now? What does that mean to us? When will the other shoe drop? The speculation goes on and on until people tire of it; finally, as we see   , people are left with one more perception or belief about the organiza.   nploys them.

This belief is neatly cat̲a̲l̲o̲g̲u̲ed and filed away with all the others and helps people develop some sense of the predictability of the organization. But notice that the whole reactive or journalistic model is a response to an event. Without the event, this reaction cannot take place. With the event, it happens almost of its own will. The momentum once begun continues until it is played out in a belief. Except for the shaping of the formal message, no one seems to manage the process particularly or to be accountable for it.

And that is one of the major defects of reactive communication as the

Figure 4.4

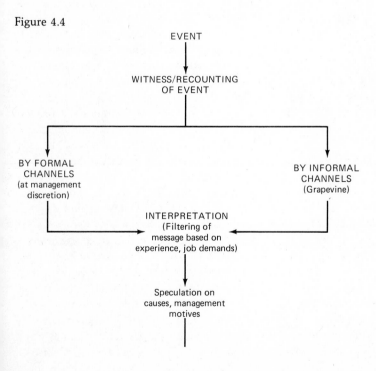

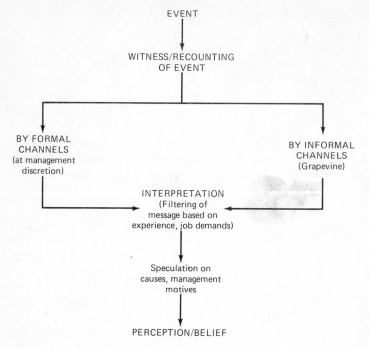

Figure 4.5

habitual way that an organization communicates to its people. It is impossible to put an end to reactive communication because there are always surprises in life, and we must explain and defend our reactions. But it is possible to stop relying on reactive communication as the primary mode for organizational communication. And in today's organization climate it is essential to do so.

Why this is so is clear from examining some of the limitations of reactive communication. To begin with, as Table 4.1 shows, reactive communication focuses mainly on *what* happened. And that's not really the major issue. In most organizations it is not difficult to find out what happened. All you have to do is keep your eyes and ears open. What is difficult is to find out why something happened. Ironically, this is what we explain least well. In fact, much of the time we simply ignore "the why" in favor of "the what." That's a poor strategy, because people want to know why more than what.

The second limitation of reactive communication is that it leaves the audience to speculate on the event's cause and significance. The danger here is that they have so little information from which to speculate intelligently. In fact, about the only real information they have is the event itself. From this information they are expected to deduce what caused the event and what it means in the scheme of things. It's not surprising that the audience is wrong a good share of the time on both counts. The problem for management is that to talk about the causes and significance of the event is to run the risk of pointing fingers at one of their own

TABLE 4.1 LIMITATIONS OF REACTIVE PROCESS

Focuses mainly on what happened

Leaves audience to speculate on event's cause and significance

Depends on audience's ability to deduce causes and motivations from event

Tends to overload audience with raw information, news, rumors, and opinions

Promotes view that organization life is chaotic, unplanned, unmanaged

Diffuses communication responsibility in the organization

or to indulge themselves in adventurous speculation. Most managements don't care for either one of these activities.

The third limitation is one of the gravest of all. It is that the reactive process in large measure depends on the audience's ability to figure out causes and management motivations by starting at the event itself and reasoning back from that event. The truth is that the audience has great difficulty doing this because, for one, business events generally have complex causes. Rarely are the events simple cause-effect relationships. Rather there is a multiplicity of interrelated causes both inside and outside the organization. The employee audience doesn't have access to all the facts, so the grapevine opts for the simplistic explanation and cheerfully spreads it around. Why did we have to recall the latest model of product Z from the marketplace? It's easy. The vice-president in charge of that project was an incompetent who skimped on quality control and reliability studies. That may or may not be true. It may also not be the real reason for the recall. But it will do until a better one comes along—probably too late to matter to anybody.

Another reason the audience has difficulty reasoning back from an event is simple distance. Anyone who has ever worked for a large organization is well aware that such organizations are status laden. The symbols—from the executive dining room to the isolated and guarded executive suite—are all over the place. Most encounters of average employees with their senior people are strictly chance, and when they happen both parties are a little uncomfortable. In fact, in some companies the senior people are mostly names on a letterhead or an organization chart.

Given that fact, how on earth can the employee audience hope to guess at management motives with much accuracy? The solution at most places is to omit motive from communication and assume that people will merely accept the announcement at face value. This is a terribly naive assumption, because the audience will always seek a management motive when one isn't given. And even when one is given, they will examine it carefully to see if they believe it. The danger in all this is that the audience is usually guessing at the motives of strangers—and powerful strangers at that. It strikes me as a dangerous game for management to play either wittingly or unwittingly.

A fourth problem making reactive communication the less desirable way to communicate in an organization is its tendency to add to the information overload that has us all reeling in both our work and private lives. It's interesting that the price of producing information has decreased dramatically in the last 50 years. In the same period distribution costs have also been reduced by a significant factor. But the cost of consuming information remains constant. It takes as long to read a page today as it did when the printing press was invented, and with so much more to read, all of us are paying dearly for the consumption of raw information.

Reactive communication tends to give us additional pieces to add to the puzzle, while doing little to help complete the puzzle. The result is that our supply of raw information, news, rumor, and opinion is merely expanded when we read the latest organizational communique.

A fifth serious limitation of the process is that it tends to be an organizational stepchild. If you look at the reactive model, it's hard to see who owns the communication process. Our instinctive tendency is to give it to senior management, because they are, after all, accountable. But given the existence of the grapevine and the likelihood that all they will be able to do is confirm or deny, they're not all that anxious to accept ownership. In fact, many members of senior management would much prefer to ignore the whole thing and let the grapevine have its way. This is obviously tempting to a harried senior executive who sees all this as a losing game, but it's far too dangerous an option. So management in most institutional organizations do the best they can, with an air of cynical resignation, believing that people will believe the worst anyway.

In some cases management wash their hands of the process and hire a professional communicator to communicate for them. This never works, because the communicator cannot be a proxy for the management. The communicator will ultimately be relegated to the role of manager of employee lip service, and no one with any integrity can last in that nonrole. I would say that the worst thing that can happen to a communication professional is to be given the keys to the communication closet.

With communication responsibility thus diffused in the reactive process, it is inevitable that it will create the impression that organization life is chaotic, unplanned, and unmanaged. Because of the tendency to communicate reactively, organizations seem to be victims of events. They respond, they parry, and they explain, but rarely do they seem to be in control. It's far from a comfortable feeling for the people who have cast their economic lot with a given company, hospital, or financial institution. I don't think it's an exaggeration to blame reactive communication for a large part of that feeling.

If reactive communication is ineffective as the primary form of organizational communication, then what's the alternative? First, let me issue the important caveat that there is no way ever to escape the reactive mode completely. There are always surprises. There are always mistakes and accidents to explain. Hence we have to be prepared to react.

But we can make our communication efforts mainly proactive, a current word coined by the futurists to remind us that we have to anticipate events and have plans in place to deal with them. In its application to organizational communication, *proactive* means mainly "issues communication." Our job is to identify, define, and articulate the major issues that the organization must address if it is to be successful.

What is an issue? Unfortunately, this is something of a dealer's choice, but the dictionary provides one helpful hint by calling it "a matter that is in dispute." In general, an *organizational issue* is any major concern that is likely to have a significant effect on the organization's ability to achieve its goals and whose outcome is in doubt.

These are the issues that constituent audiences, whether they are employees or shareholders or government agencies, want to hear about and talk about. And the audience wants to know early in the life of the issue, not when it has fixed its grip on the organization and is threatening to do it serious harm.

Like reactive communication, proactive communication can be modeled so that it is a relatively simple process to understand. Any management that wants to do good issues communication, which is another way of saying proactive communication, must begin the process with an honest and thorough assessment of where the organization is today. The process is a sizing up process and can be done in any way management chooses so long as it is objective and reasonably complete.

As we see in Figure 4.6, the probable sources for the assessment of any organization are many and varied. One of the first places to look is at the organization's long-range plan. This can be a gold mine of goals, objectives, risks, and exposures—if it is well done. It should go a long way toward revealing where management hopes to take the organization and what it sees as some of the obstacles along the way.

The annual operating plan is likewise an excellent source of where the organization needs and wants to go in the shorter term. Because it is looking at a more predictable business environment, the annual operating plan tends to be more focused and realistic about the organization's prospects.

A third excellent source of information for assessing one's organization is interviews with senior executives. The question is what they aspire to in their own area of the business and what they see as the major impediments to getting there, in both the short and long term.

Figure 4.6

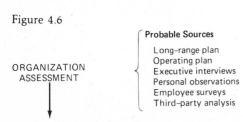

ORGANIZATION
ASSESSMENT

Probable Sources

Long-range plan
Operating plan
Executive interviews
Personal observations
Employee surveys
Third–party analysis

Personal observations of the person doing the assessment should also carry considerable weight so long as that person has been around long enough to have formed some valid impressions. And they should certainly be thrown into the hopper along with all the other assessment material.

A more objective assessment can also be bought from an astute consultant who is hired to look at the business and in his or her expert opinion size up management and employee aspirations as well as potential. Such third-party analyses, along with unsolicited analyses from investment experts and securities analysts, can be invaluable.

Actually, the sources for a good organization assessment are as varied and as broad as the imagination of the people who are doing the assessing. Everything that helps to capture the reality of that particular organization's personality, strength, and weaknesses should be thrown into the pot. The product should then be a stew that simmers endlessly, with new ingredients added as the organization changes. That's an important point, since no living organization stands still, and an assessment once done must be modified as time and circumstances require.

The next step in proactive communication planning, as shown in Figure 4.7, is to face a question that most organizations tend to ignore—why are we investing time and resources in the communication process? What return do we expect to achieve on this investment? Why is this trip necessary? Frequently, the assumptions are implicit rather than explicit. We all "know" that we are communicating to recognize people's contributions and to motivate them; we all "know" that we are trying to improve morale through better information; we all "know" that we are attempting to win employee support for business goals and strategy, and on and on. But do we really know? Are those the assumptions of senior management about communication? Are those the assumptions of the professional communication people? Do they really believe those things will be the outcome? If they do, how do they know?

The task here obviously is to develop a joint set of assumptions about the probable effects of good communication practice in the organization. What are

Figure 4.7

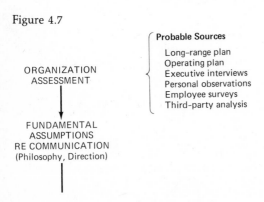

a reasonable set of expected outcomes if we could magically begin doing all the right things tomorrow? It is vital to articulate those assumptions and to agree that this is what we mutually have a right to expect from the process. Otherwise, no one really knows why we have launched this bewildering process and what we should be looking for at the other end. And certainly this is the time to get rid of unrealistic or impossible views of what communication alone can accomplish in and for the organization.

Once the fundamental assumptions are developed by the communicator and agreed to by the senior executive of the organization, it is possible, and indeed essential, to begin developing both the program and content strategies that will be required. In our model of proactive communication in Figure 4.8, the program strategy is shown on the left side. The content strategy (Figure 4.9) is on the right side. Program and content strategy are parallel tasks in the sense that in formulating the organization assessment and in setting up fundamental assumptions about communication in the organization, the communicator will uncover issues and think about how to deliver them in convincing terms. But inevitably he or she will also think about appropriate communication programs to deliver the issues.

Having said that, for the sake of our proactive model, we will pretend that

Figure 4.8

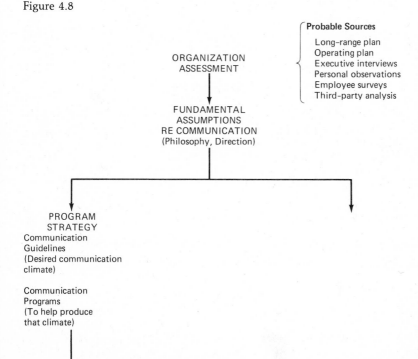

the process is mainly serial. When the organization assessment has been carefully and painstakingly thought through and the fundamental assumptions have been agreed to, the next logical step is to develop communication guidelines for everyone to live by. Like the Xerox guidelines on page 38, these guidelines should articulate the role and responsibility of management in the communication process for the simple reason that management has the accountability.

The guidelines keep everyone honest by spelling out where communication responsibility lies and how it should be carried out. Ideally, such guidelines should be pronounced from the very top of the organization and endorsed at every key level. Once this happens, the next step is to weave the guidelines into the institutional framework of the organization. In Xerox, for example, the guidelines were spelled out in the employee handbook for everyone to see as a commitment to the ideal of effective information exchange within the company. They were also held up as the justification for plans and programs to improve the employee communication process in Xerox.

This brings us to our next point. If the guidelines flow from the fundamental assumptions about communication and represent the direction the organization plans to take in its proactive communication strategy, the next step is to develop the communication programs that will be necessary to make those guidelines come alive or, when such programs already exist, to be certain that they are good enough to carry the freight they will need to. What freight is that? It is the issues that need to be communicated both inside and outside the organization.

In my 20-plus years in organizational communication, I have shuddered at the slapdash way in which key communication programs are conceived and introduced. In more cases than I can count, some neglected and naive communication specialist decides that he or she would like to work with such and such a medium, researches it briefly, and presents a proposal detailing all the alleged benefits to the organization. The truth is that too often this person would dearly love to edit a four-color slick magazine or to produce videocassette recordings with the financial backing of his or her management. Will such a program really move the organization closer to its goals, or is it a toy or an ego piece that is largely a waste of company resources? In the absence of good communication planning, no one knows, because no one is sure of what the outcomes should be anyway.

And this brings us to the other side of the proactive model in Figure 4.9. Under the heading "Content Strategy," there are two main tasks. The first is the development of a message platform, which is merely a handy label to describe the issues that have been selected as the key ones to be communicated to particular constituencies. Like the planks in a political platform, the issues are selected carefully and become the foundation on which the organization builds its various positions. These positions are mainly the proposed management solutions and strategies for dealing with the issues that surface in the organization assessment.

What, for example, does the organization want and need to do about becoming more cost effective? What is the basic business strategy for dealing with

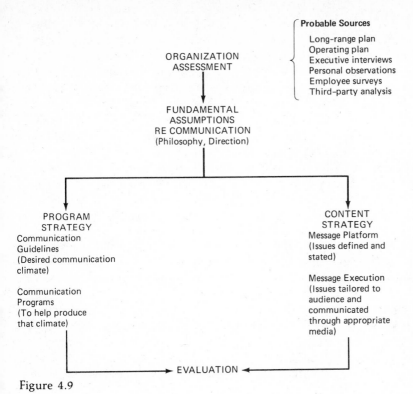

Figure 4.9

skillful competition? How about human productivity and its role in helping alleviate the ravages of inflation? Where does the company stand on affirmative action and equal opportunity and what is being done about the two? And, the questioning goes on until the major issues of concern to management and employee alike are transformed into messages.

The task at this point of the model is to select the issues of major importance to the organization, set them up in some kind of priority list, and then use them to drive the content of every one of the organization's communication programs. This is the second main task under content strategy—message execution—and it is here, of course, that the proactive communication program either lapses into a tired recitation of private enterprise pieties and me-too positions or becomes alive with honest and gutsy statements and positions the audience can relate to.

It is here that we worry about the needs and interests of the particular audience we must reach—whether employees, shareholders, customers, citizens of the community in which the organization does business, or perhaps government regulatory bodies. This process, of course, requires us to tailor the message and determine which issues are important to whom.

The final process in the proactive model is evaluation—a difficult process that does not normally yield much objective data. Nonetheless, it is imperative for the communicator to use every technique he or she can dream up to measure the effectiveness of the process—employee attitude surveys, broad communication surveys, readership surveys, interviews, or anything else that can be devised to determine what is or is not working when measured against the original assumptions about communication in a given organization.

What are some of the major advantages of proactive issues communication? There are many. First, as Table 4.2 suggests, the process tends to identify the organization's concerns and priorities and to indicate what management proposes to do about them. This process is reassuring, because employees particularly know what they are experiencing in the way of day-to-day problems. If they never see those things acknowledged as problems or if they hear no talk of possible solutions, they become anxious. They fear management is simply not on top of things.

A second advantage of the proactive process is that it focuses on the significance of events rather than their mere occurrence. This is extremely important, because what people want to know is "What does the event mean?" The event's occurrence is common knowledge.

A third advantage is that the proactive process tends to provide a frame of reference in which particular events can be placed and explained: "Yes, this may be a setback, but, no, it is not a disaster. Remember we told you that one of the tough issues we were up against this year was . . ." In this fashion it is possible to provide a sense of proportion and order and to convey the feeling that someone is indeed in charge.

A fourth advantage of the process is that it can be used to foreshadow change and provide justification for the change. Because of a particular issue, an organization may have to take actions that look extraordinary or poorly conceived when viewed in isolation. But when the actions can be explained in light of certain issues or needs, they can begin to make very good sense. In the process, people can be

TABLE 4.2 ADVANTAGES OF PROACTIVE COMMUNICATION PLANNING PROCESS (FOR AUDIENCE)

Identifies organization's concerns and priorities

Focuses on significance of events rather than on their mere occurrence

Provides perspective and sense of order

Foreshadows change and provides justification

Fosters "connectedness" of events and sense that one's work life has meaning

Pressures leadership to match words with actions

Encourages hope and optimism

prepared to adapt to changes that would otherwise be passively or actively resisted.

Similarly, good proactive communication tends to make the organization look like a rational universe in which one's work life has meaning. Given the values and needs of today's worker, this is a significant advantage. Proactive issues once communicated are a course the organization will try to steer by. There will be an attempt to match words and actions, and changes will be made deliberately and in response to other issues, not capriciously. The end result, I believe, of this kind of rational universe is a more hopeful and optimistic work force.

There is an excellent chance that people who are hopeful and optimistic, if their hope and optimism turn out to be well founded, will be more productive and more committed. This is a hard statement to prove, but common sense suggests that it's true.

What are some of the advantages of proactive communication for the professional communicator?

First, for the communication staff, this disciplined approach to communication carries their effort to organization issues and priorities. In no time it is clear to management that the communicators are no longer working the other side of the street, that they are indeed concerned about the very matters of concern to senior management. The inevitable result is that the communicators get greater attention and support from their own management.

Second, this process has the advantage of helping the communicator to understand better that the job is not journalism or publishing. The job is organizational communication, and the communicator's journalistic or publication skills are critical but incidental to the task of organizational communication.

Third, proactive communication influences the content of communication and disciplines the very process so that the professional communicator is not merely pursuing the subjects and issues that excite him or her.

Fourth, because the process requires careful evaluation and analysis of issues, it helps to insure that communication is an honest process matched to both management and audience needs. Issues are not merely top down. They also become bottom up as the communicator attempts to determine the concerns and information needs of the audience.

There are also significant advantages for management in the proactive approach to communication. For one, communication becomes a planned process rather than an afterthought or an attempt to explain what went wrong or to defend why something was done. In this manner the reactions of various constituencies are anticipated and addressed as the policy or program is being implemented. In short, communication is a planned part of the management process.

In the next chapter, let's reduce all this to practice in another fictional company to see how the process can actually be managed to alter ineffective and inefficient communication practices.

NOTES

1. Jerry B. Harvey, "The Abilene Paradox: The Management of Agreement," *Organizational Dynamics*, Summer 1974, pp. 63–80.
2. M. R. Cooper, B. S. Morgan, P. M. Foley, and L. B. Kaplan, "Changing Employee Values: Deepening Discontent?" *Harvard Business Review*, January–February 1979, pp. 124–125.

Chapter 5

A Case History in Proactive Employee Communication

The public media should represent for us in organizational communication an interesting case study of how not to do our jobs. I say this because, by definition, the public media are the classic example of reactive communication: they react to the events in the news and report them—warts and all—to the public, who must then assemble the information into some sort of coherent picture of life in contemporary times.

The problem generally lies with what we define as an event. In Western society an event, if we judge from the content of the media, is very simple. It is any startling, shocking, worrisome, or unnerving happening that can be capsulized and aimed at us from a television screen or newspaper page. Such events are occasionally laced with a hopeful note or a passing example of human concern or caring, but the preponderance of what the public media feed us is negative stuff. As an audience we are often left with a sense of confusion and even despair. Will there be peace in the Middle East, or is war about to break out? Yesterday's report, like yesterday's weather, said one thing. Today's says another. What do we believe? Is anyone in control? Because this issue could be the subject of a book itself, we'll not examine it further here.

The subject, however, is important to organizational communicators, because most of them look for their role models in public journalism. Roger Mudd and Dan Rather report the news. The editorial staffs of the *New York Times* and the *Wall Street Journal* do the same. Hence, since we are writers and media people mainly, that's probably about what we should do. It's so tempting, but it's also so wrong.

All this is compounded because management usually does not understand how to manage communication people. Without proper direction and with no direct link to the organization's products or services, communication people grope in frustration for a proper role model. Time and time again I have heard the wish expressed that the employee communication professional ought to be free to perform his or her job in the same way that the press is free to do its job in the society at large. This is utter nonsense, but it remains the secret hope of many of my colleagues in this business.

The result is that these communicators act out a needless and hopeless effort to get their management "to tell employees the truth." They conceive of themselves as newspaper reporters or crusading editors and publishers with the power and rights of the press behind them. No management in its right mind is going to use company funds to finance such an enterprise.

The problem is not management's penchant for deceit or desire to cover up. It is a rightful concern about what raw, unprocessed information does to or for an employee audience. This is difficult, if not impossible, to predict. It is also why so many organization management teams are nervous about the mere reportage of organization news without putting it into some kind of perspective for the audience. Management likes news to have a beginning, a middle, and some probable, predictable outcome before it is ready to say much about it. It also wants to present its actions and performance in some kind of favorable light. This is not an unusual human desire.

It seems to me that the role of doing otherwise should not logically fall to communication people who draw their salary from the organization. That altogether proper role belongs historically and correctly to the public press. In fact, the organizational communicator who models his or her work and aspirations on the media is doomed to a career of frustration and loneliness.

In fairness, the opposite extreme has been even more typical of corporate communication. The old-time house organ "where never is heard a discouraging word and the skies are not cloudy all day" was fully as unsatisfactory as the emerging hope that organizational communicators should be investigative reporters in their own establishments. In both instances the models are wrong, and the results are likely to be disastrous.

To better understand the point let's look at another fictional outfit called United Industries. United originally made its name in the oil business. In the 1960s it nervously acquired three other large organizations to protect its base. With the onset of the energy crisis in the early 1970s, it began to take more than a passing interest in the other nonpetroleum companies. One was a television and motion picture production outfit; the second, a chemical company, and the third, a manufacturer of air conditioners.

When United finally was able to build a management organization to direct the activities of its conglomerate operations, it set up its corporate headquarters in neutral territory in San Diego. As part of this effort, Otto Baumgarten, president of United, appointed a vice-president of corporate communication to insure that the world understood exactly what United was and what it was doing in the business world. Massive sums of money were pumped into television advertising and paid-space think pieces in the nation's leading magazines and newspapers. In 1971 the new vice-president decided something had to be done about the company's creaking house organ that had been published monthly under the predictable name of *Folks United.* When there was only the relatively small oil business located mainly in the Southwest, FU, as the jaded staffers tagged it, was able to do a reasonable job of reporting the bond drives, engagements, birthdays, new hires, activities of the United Recreation Association, employee hobbies, and the like.

But as United grew from its employee base of 2000 or 3000 people who worked within a few miles of one another, FU began to look sillier and sillier—especially to the employees of the television and motion picture division, who used to sit around and mock the names and activities of their fellow employees from the oil fields. When *Folks United* arrived in the mail, it was always the occasion for lots of merriment and what was called the continuing saga of John Bob and Willie Joe. It wasn't much better at Koolking Air Conditioning, whose production people every month sent their stack of copies unread to shipping to be used as packing and wrapping material.

When Bart Damon was hired as employee communication manager, he was instructed to bring this thing into the twentieth century and build an appropriate communication program for all of United so that its internal efforts would be as sophisticated as its external efforts. Damon's first move was to begin assembling a staff. He began by hiring the business editor of one of southern California's major newspapers. Next he found and hired an outstanding writer who had been free-lancing in New York with considerable success. Damon's third hire was an audiovisual manager from Hollywood Productions Unlimited. The rest of the staff consisted of the former staff of FU and the communication people who had been in place at the chemical division and Koolking Air Conditioning.

The early days of Damon's regime were very exciting, as the new staff eagerly planned their respective publications and programs and turned them from concept to reality. *Folks United* was turned into a weekly "newspaper" in tabloid form and rechristened *United Industries News.* It was to be the showpiece of the effort and was to be used to keep all United people informed of all news affecting them and their work. Dick Larkspur, the former newsman, was named editor and given free rein to report the news. New York free-lancer Gabe Newcomb was given the job of producing a management magazine to be circulated to all United managers and to reflect the strategy and priorities of United management.

After six months, the honeymoon came to an abrupt halt. Larkspur had produced a series on the disruption caused families of United employees who had been transferred from the Southwest to the West Coast to the East Coast, and in some cases to the Middle East and back. It was a frank story, complete with bitter complaints and heartrending histories of uprooted wives and children. There was little, if any, expression of the stiff-upper-lip philosophy that corporate families are supposed to espouse, and Sheldon Horowitz, marketing vice-president, was furious when the first of the series appeared. He called Larkspur, screamed a string of obscenities at him and, after more sputtering about whether he thought he was Woodward or Bernstein, demanded that he kill the series. Then he hung up on a dazed Larkspur before the editor had a chance to reply.

Through a series of skillful negotiations, Damon was able to keep the series from an untimely and abrupt death. But this was the beginning of a gradual polarization of United management, on the one hand, and United communication people, on the other. It has been fueled many times over by haggling over stories, communication proposals, and even the last-minute killing of the whole issue of a given publication.

Poor Damon is caught in the middle of this continuing conflict between his staff, who constantly confront him with their views that United people have a need and a right to know what is going on in the company and outside the company, and his management's accusations that "these people have no understanding of the sensitivities of this business." Damon's plight is compounded by his own sympathy with his staff's beliefs and his journalistic training—all of which say to him that United management is too conservative and too worried about reactions that will never materialize.

On top of this Bart Damon himself is 33 years old, a Vietnam veteran, and a product of the campus upheaval of the class of '69. He confides to his friends that he is not all that pleased about working for a company like United, but the money is excellent and he lives well. Damon's peers in the communication profession rate *United Industries News* as one of the top 10 company publications in the United States. In professional competitions it continually walks off with prizes for its candor and excellence.

So what's the problem? It's one that isn't spoken of much outside the gatherings of people who make their livings from organizational communication. But it's classic. The United communication staff is doing its own thing in the organization—writing the kinds of things *they* care about, quietly jabbing and prodding their own management, and producing publications and programs that are professionally satisfying for *them* to work on. Because the programs are mostly of reasonable quality and because management honestly does not know how to get hold of the reins, they do what they like, more or less. The one exception is management's right to review content, and this right is exercised with some relish.

The one question that does not get raised, let alone answered, is "What is all this activity doing for United and for United Industries people?" The classic answer from the communication people is a soft-shoe dance. "Well, you know there is really no objective way you can measure the effect of communication . . . . Next question?"

Is there an alternative to this scenario? Until recently most communication people thought the alternative was for them simply to serve their employers as hired guns, grinding out copy they didn't believe and finding the right sugarcoating for the "truths" management wanted people to swallow. It's a depressing alternative, and it's no surprise that the people who opted for it are disenchanted and cynical. It's also no surprise that the Bart Damons of the world are trying to walk a very different road. But the role of corporate conscience and self-appointed purveyor of the truth is a thankless and often arrogant one.

In my view the answer is for the communicator to lead the way in making communication in his or her organization proactive. By this I mean that the communicator can no longer afford the waiting game in which he or she expects management to define the communication task and then provide the money and psychic support to do the job. Because there has largely been communication anarchy in our organizations, this has been the traditional approach to the problem. When management finally ignores the communication function or perhaps emasculates it because the senior staff can't figure out how to work effectively with this alien breed, the predictable result is that the professional communicators sulk, sink into despair, or "give them what they want." In all three cases the organization is the loser.

The solution lies in what any intelligent staff person must do in any organization. It requires communication people to think through the organization's needs, assess their potential ability to help address those needs, propose an intelligent, carefully thought-through plan, and then execute it as professionally as they know how. No sulking, no bitterness, no lamentation about not being understood or appreciated. These are all beside the point—which is this: How to do the job as intelligently and effectively as possible.

Proactive communication requires the communication professional to see himself or herself in a different role from that of the working journalist. Although it's probably one of the more distasteful words in our vocabulary, the literal word for describing a proactive communicator is *propagandist.* The trouble with the word is that it conjures up visions of twisting the truth and the reality of our lives into lies serving the interests of certain special interest groups only. This is the commonly accepted notion of propaganda, for the simple reason that the opponents of a given idea, cause, or institution have always found it convenient to use the word as a disparaging label.

Those of us in organizations always carry this burden, whether we pose as independent journalists or as company spokesmen. Our various audiences invariably filter our messages, words, and claims through their belief that we are paid to say these things. The truth is that we are. But it is true also that the most believable propaganda is the truth. Ergo the good communicators among us rely on truth rather than lies to influence opinions and attitudes. More to the point, the ethical communicator will decline to lie for anyone, since this is prostitution.

All this requires that people who cast their lot with organizations as organizational communicators had also better be smart and have well-formed consciences. If not, they are frequently in danger of compromising however much integrity they have. This is a subject well beyond the scope of this book, but it is one that requires sober personal reflection.

Organizations will always propagandize, just as all of us individually propagandize about ourselves. We always seek noble explanations for our actions. We always try to put ourselves and our behavior in the most acceptable light.

Since this kind of behavior is both inevitable and vital to the survival and well-being of the organization, the real question becomes "How can any management and its communication staff communicate as decently, truthfully, and effectively as possible?" I think this is the question because it seems to me the communicator's responsibility is complex. The responsibility is to the well-being of the organization first, the audience second, and society at large third. I am also prepared to believe that in some cases these priorities can shift. To cite an extreme, I believe that Daniel Ellsberg was right to release the Pentagon Papers to the *New York Times.* Ellsberg's first obligation in this case, it seems to me, was to the American people rather than to the Pentagon or to President Nixon.

The proactive communication process is based on the assumption that organizations spend much of their time and energy trying to meet certain objectives they have set for themselves. In accomplishing these objectives they invariably are required to identify, confront, and solve problems that they rate in some priority fashion. Priority normally is determined by how much influence any given problem is likely to have on the accomplishment of important organization objectives.

The dynamics of this situation are the raw material of real organizational communication. They are the substance that employees want and need to understand if they are to give their most creative and most-enlightened effort to the work organization.

Let's take another look at Bart Damon and see what he might have done differently if he had tried to establish a proactive communication program at United. The first step he should have taken was to assess the communication climate at United when he was hired. There are many ways to do this, but one of the best is to hire a perceptive and reliable outsider to survey the audience. Damon could do this himself, but the truth is that third parties frequently have more credibility than in-house talent. It is the old story of the prophet without honor in his own country; most management teams will pay more attention to an assessment or a survey prepared by someone whom they see as being objective.

A sadder but wiser Damon could start with such a survey. Let's say he simply finds a good consultant who will sit small representative groups (10–12 people) down in each of the four divisions of the company and walk them through a structured discussion to find out what they like about how they're communicated with and what they don't like. If he speaks to enough of these groups—say, four or five in each division—he will soon have a good understanding of what people want to know about and why. Armed with this feedback, he can put together a statement of where United is today and where it probably needs to go.

Let's assume that the outcome of such a discussion yields the following findings (and these, incidentally, are not atypical of large organizations).

- First, United people are concerned mainly with what is going on in their own divisions. They care about the overall picture of United and its well-being but mainly want to know about their own operating division. In the survey they say that they have considerable difficulty finding out such information.

- Second, they complain that they hear lots about how tough the market-place is in chemicals and air conditioning and that they are tired of all the static they get from people who somehow blame them personally for the price of oil, but they don't understand United's business strategy. What are the main priorities of the business? How will management determine satisfactory corporate performance? What are the major obstacles to success in each division, and how does management propose to overcome them?

- Third, they resent having to get most of their information about what is going on in United from the grapevine. They lament that no one tells them anything officially. It's like pulling teeth to get any information from their immediate bosses, who claim to be as much in the dark as they are.

- Fourth, they claim that United does not care much about its people or have much respect for their abilities. They say that management mouths lots of pieties about people being their greatest asset, but they don't think anyone in management really believes that.

- Fifth, they say that they are generally interested in helping United do better. They care about the company's future, but they are frustrated because no one ever asks for their ideas, and, in fact, when they do make suggestions, no one seems too anxious to hear them or act on them.

- Sixth, when asked which information source they prefer to hear from, the majority say their immediate supervisor. The reason is simple. The employees know their supervisors and have the opportunity to ask questions.

When Damon pieces together the consultant's report and begins reflecting on it, he sees several important needs emerging.

- First, people want business information. They stated clearly that they aren't much interested in chitchat about their fellow employees.

- Second, they want to know first about the condition of their own divisions. How is a division doing now? What are the prospects for the future? What can the employees do personally to make their division stronger and more secure?

- Third, it is clear that people want some face-to-face dialogue with the boss. They want to be able to raise their questions and get honest answers, and they want to influence the boss's decisions about the work.

- Fourth, managers need both information and training if they are to communicate better with their people. For now, they don't know if United wants them to communicate with their people. No one has ever trusted the managers to pass along important information, which is usually posted on bulletin boards and published in the company newspaper.

All this taken together is the first step Damon will make in beginning the process of an organization assessment of United Industries.

Step two is to begin interviewing each of the United division presidents to get their individual perspectives on their own parts of the business as well as their views of how their divisions fit into the whole. The results of these interviews will prove interesting and unsettling to Damon, who, for example, will find that the television and motion picture division is hanging on by its fingernails. Max Boroshevsky, division president, has confided that unless the division can make a record profit on its new television movie, it is certain that there will be serious layoffs and that the division might even fold. The problem is that rising production costs and talent fees are making it almost impossible to record a decent profit. Division employees have little idea just how serious the situation is, although there have been rumors of financial trouble.

Boroshevsky himself has always been a high liver and is most reluctant to cut back on the privileges that his creative people have traditionally enjoyed since before United acquired them in the 1970s. The possibility of admitting the problems publicly makes Boroshevsky very nervous.

In the chemicals division, it is another story. Ed Pringle, division president, grew up in the chemicals business. He has always been one of the industry's sharpest production people, managing the business conservatively and with a careful eye to the bottom line. Although the business has been under some cost pressure in the last two or three years, he has invested capital wisely in production equipment and has put profit back into research. The result is that the division's profit and loss statement is in excellent shape. The only trouble is that profit problems in motion pictures and air conditioning have put what Pringle regards as unreasonable demands on his division for profit performance. Pringle is an old-time, bull-of-the-woods manager and has serious reservations about whether his people need to be communicated with. He summed up his philosophy in a comment to Damon: "Look, all these people really want is a secure job. They don't give a hoot about United or the chemical business if their jobs are safe. So don't bother me with all this communication crap."

Calvin Putnam is the colorful president of Koolking Air Conditioning in Pennsylvania. He rose through the sales organization and will do anything to spur his salespeople on. Koolking dealers can't believe that this wise-cracking, fast-talking character is a corporate executive. They love the man but can't imagine how he fits into an organization like United Industries. At the last dealer convention, Putnam appeared in a Superman suit and helped act out a skit in which Koolking Air Conditioners beat the Heat and Humidity Bandits.

Putnam's employees are a bit less taken with him than the Koolking dealers. In fact, one Putnam district sales manager told Damon when he was visiting sales offices, "Whatever you do, keep that clown Putnam out of the field offices. All he ever does when he comes here is stir up trouble for local management to deal with. He's an insensitive clod."

The petroleum division, which was the forerunner of United Industries, is predictably the most staid of all the United divisions. It is enormously profitable as a consequence of the rising price of oil, but it is under the same pressures as other oil companies to find new energy sources. The result is that the petroleum division is spending most of its time and energy in research and development and in trying to market a scarce commodity prudently. Of all the divisions, petroleum is the most paternalistic and, in many respects, the least communicative. The one exception is the division's active program to turn public opinion in its favor against government regulation of industry in general and the energy industry in particular.

Faced with this mixture of organizational styles, problems, and personalities, and a strong divisional tradition of autonomy, Damon begins working out the logical assumptions that can be made about the proper role of communication in the business. From his original assessment, he concludes that several assumptions need to be articulated and reviewed with his own management:

- First, divisional autonomy is so well entrenched and so important that no communication program will work unless it is owned and supported in the operating divisions. It cannot be simply mandated from United headquarters.
- Second, there are two sets of business issues in United. One is the overall needs of United as a collection of divisions. The other is the various business issues peculiar to each division as a function of the separate industries they are in.
- Third, people in the divisions care most about what is happening in their own backyards. United is real to them as a company and as the source of their benefits, but they know that their fates are tied up with the performance of their own divisions.
- Fourth, United is so diverse that its various employee audiences need to be carefully identified and communicated with according to their particular needs. The engineers, for example, need one kind of communication, the sales force another, and the production people still another.
- Fifth, there is a clear and slightly different need in all the divisions for improved employee communication. The universal subjects of competition, turnover, increasing costs, and declining productivity need to be addressed so that United people better understand what is expected of them.
- Sixth, the communication process at United can be humanized and made a two-way, interactive process only through the human presence of

United managers. Somehow, the managers will have to be shown the need, given whatever training is necessary, and be held accountable for effective communication with their people.

- Seventh, better-informed United people who identified their self-interests with the business would very likely be more productive and more committed employees.

- Eighth, not all problems are rooted in communication failures; what may look like a communication failure may instead be a case of management's communicating a message in its actions that overrode its words. The point here is that actions and words must be consistent if the United communication programs are to be credible.

From this set of assumptions, Damon next works with his own staff and the divisional staff to develop a set of guidelines for effective employee communication in each division, regardless of the values, personality, or style of divisional leadership. Percival Hand, United chairman, is very much behind this strategy, since he is well aware that divisional autonomy has perhaps gone too far in the recent past. There are numerous guidelines in the final proposal that Damon makes to the management committee of United, but they amount to three basic principles:

- Employee communication in the divisions is not an option. It is the right of the employees and the responsibility of division management, a responsibility that will be evaluated by the corporate staff and part of local management's performance review.

- Division management will fund and manage an appropriate set of communication media that will be monitored by the corporate staff for quality, relevance, and timeliness. The media will focus on division business issues.

- Managers at United will be expected to polish their communication skills with their people so that they are the primary company information sources. To this end, there will be training and improved information programs for managers, whose communication activity will be measured in their performance reviews.

With the guidelines established and endorsed by the United management committee, Damon next works with division management to be certain that their various employee audiences are identified carefully. Employee communication programs, including divisional publications, management newsletters, employee communication meetings with functional vice-presidents, news bulletins, appropriate complaint and suggestion programs, and the like, are all installed in the divisions as part of a communication initiative. A particular effort is made to give managers training in how to run effective meetings and what their people need in the way of information. At the corporate level, an effort is made merely to focus on the larger picture of United through such media as a corporate newsletter that everyone receives monthly, a president's newsletter to all United managers, and an occasional videotape shown to all United people. All these United media together focus on the major issues of the business with the heaviest emphasis on divisional concerns.

Damon works closely with the staff person responsible for employee communication at each division to be certain issues are properly identified for that division and to be certain the issues drive the content of the employee media. All news is communicated through a simple bulletin board system, whereby significant company news is posted routinely under the heading "News Flashes" on company bulletin boards.

The major focus of the corporate effort is to help all United people understand why the company must achieve certain stated strategic goals and the obstacles to success. Divisional issues are always related to that larger corporate strategic framework. The result is that most United people in time will have a renewed understanding of where United is going and how it will get there. Because the communication guidelines are guidelines, all four of the divisions have considerable autonomy in execution to meet their local needs and conditions. The one proviso is that they *will* meet those needs.

Damon and his staff spend much of their time coordinating their work with the divisional communication people, who for the most part are not highly skilled communication professionals because the divisions can't afford expensive programs and staff. The happy result is that a good share of the burden for effective communication falls where it belongs—on divisional management. About the only professionally produced pieces are the divisional publications, which are modest newsletters in most cases.

What are the benefits of this kind of systematic approach to communication? There are many, but the main one is that the communication effort is shaped by an overriding purpose and is not merely driven willy-nilly by the random thoughts and observations of anyone in a position of power or influence. Instead, there is the systematic communication of issues that bear on the organization's survival and well-being now and in the foreseeable future.

Further, the approach is disciplined. The communication process in most organizations is almost an afterthought. No one seems to be accountable or in control, and the result is that communication often seems to be defensive, apologetic, or incomplete. In today's fast-moving institutional world, such communication is unacceptable to the people who must do the work. They want more evidence of planning, forethought, and good management in the organization. They also want evidence of rational decision making that considers all the forces needing to be kept in balance by the organization's leadership.

When they don't see this evidence, they naturally conclude that the organization is run only with an eye on short-term results and goals. In today's world, everyone wonders if that is not courting disaster.

In our fictional United Industries, Damon will discover in time that the proactive approach to the communication process has put him and his staff more and more into the mainstream of the business. Unlike the old days when he was often the uncomfortable mediator between a senior manager and one of his miffed editors who was pursuing a news story no one was particularly anxious to report, Damon now finds that his people and he are seen more as allies than as foes.

The subjects Damon and his staff are communicating are clearly the issues of concern for the whole organization. Little by little as issues are explored, he finds a growing willingness on the part of United management to come to grips with the issues in print, on videotape, and in employee meetings. The result, ironically, is that United publications and United's other communication programs are more interesting, candid, and relevant than they ever were when the staff saw themselves purely as journalists.

Another interesting thing is happening. As United management wrestles with actions or issues that they suspect will unsettle United employees, they are seeking Damon's counsel. When should we communicate this? How should we do it? Is there any way to allay people's fears and soften some of the impact? In the old days, no one considered such matters. Management simply kept their plans under wraps until they were ready to act, and then they issued a stiff and incomplete explanation to the public media. United people got their first inkling from the newspaper or television, and there was perhaps a cursory mention in the company paper some days or weeks later. What information meant was left up to the employees to decide. Predictably, the employees' version almost always cast United management in an unfavorable light.

The final step in Damon's communication plan is to tackle the complex business of the individual manager's communication role. It turns out that United managers had never been told that this was a priority responsibility until the communication guidelines were issued. Even then, the managers tended to regard the guidelines as mostly window dressing that senior management was not serious about.

Damon had discussed the problem with United managers, and he heard the familiar protests: I don't have time for that stuff; half the time I don't know what's going on myself; when I see my boss act like that, then I'll start doing it; that's not what I'm paid for; I'm a boss, not a nursemaid; there's no reward for good communicators, only for good performers, and so forth.

The more Damon examined the problem, the more convinced he became that at United it was mainly an accountability issue. Make the manager clearly accountable, and he or she will pay some attention to the task.

Damon's interest in the problem led him to begin discussions with United's vice-president for human resources. Eventually, the two agreed that what was needed was to make this task a measure of accountability for each United manager. In turn, this eventually led to a redesign of the United performance appraisal for all managers so that a fixed percentage of their performance review would be based on their attention to communication with their people. This, in turn, would be assessed by means of a brief survey form which every manager was required to give to his or her people at performance review time.

The employees answered a set of questions about the manager's communication behavior and sent the form to human resources for scoring. The results were tabulated and reported to the manager's boss, who used them to assess the individual manager's communication efforts during the review period.

This simple device, coupled with the requirement that all operating plans had to include an employee communication strategy, subject to quarterly progress reviews, will soon make a dramatic and evident difference at United—at least in terms of management interest in communication with United people.

The proactive process that we are looking at in this case history will no doubt be time consuming and evolutionary. There will also be considerable trial and error, because these are mostly uncharted waters. But the potential payoff is enormous. If we succeed, there is an excellent chance that we can transform our various organizations into more habitable human environments that nurture creativity and innovation.

If we fail, I fear that we are doomed to live out our work existence in mindless, mainly bureaucratic organizations that stumble from crisis to crisis as their members look on helplessly and indifferently. For the truth is that today's employees will contribute on their own terms, and a great deal of that contribution depends very simply on how well they are treated and managed.

Chapter 6

The Employee Communicator's Agenda

At this writing it is clear that the leadership of our institutional organizations need help in communicating their objectives and needs to today's employees. Who is going to provide that help is not as clear. One scenario has the legal community as the likeliest candidate. Accordingly, the corporate lawyers of the world will occupy the office next door to the president and advise him or her about exactly what should and should not be said to whom. It is a cautious approach that sees presidents as increasingly beleaguered and litigated.

Another scenario claims that the computer specialists of the world own the transmission lines for most institutional information and that, therefore, they should be the ones to decide what is said to whom and when and how it should be said. Implicit in this scenario is the notion that the major problem is speedy and efficient transmission of quantitative information and that the problem can be resolved by putting lots of computer terminals and cathode ray tubes in the hands of people, who will then communicate better.

Historically, senior management has not had to worry much about the communication process. When autocratic management was the order of the day, one did not worry very much about how effective the communication process was, except in terms of whether people understood orders. When management did begin to worry about such things, as the times and audiences changed, they simply did what they had always done and turned to their close staff advisers. The trouble is that these staffs have been organized according to special disciplines—personnel, finance, marketing, manufacturing, legal, and the like. To whom does one turn when the problem is communication? It's been a dealer's choice, with public relations (in those companies large enough to have the function) the typical choice.

The public relations people have usually focused their attention outside the organization toward the news media, shareholders, or financial community. More often than not, the role of public relations has been to react to the needs of such consituencies without much thought for the employees of the organization. When a deliberate attempt was made to communicate to the employees, the senior executive usually turned to personnel.

And therein lies one of today's organizational problems that is not well understood. Good communication is so closely allied to good management that it is very difficult to carve it up into neat organizational pieces. It's too pervasive a process to permit that. It cuts back and forth across organizational lines, and it becomes difficult for senior management to know where to go for help.

The problem is compounded further by the confusion over where the employee communication professionals should report. According to one school of thought, since these professionals work as writers, editors, and publishers of company media, they naturally belong with their kind in public relations; another school of thought says they communicate company information to company employees—logically a personnel activity—and thus should be part of the personnel structure.

In most organizations the result has been a custody fight. Like most custody fights, it has not been particularly pleasant for any of the parties. The big loser, in my estimation, has been the organization. The other big loser has been the communicators, who have not been given the direction, opportunity, and attention they need to do the complex job that has to be done.

The two toughest questions for people in organizational communication have been these: "Who am I?" And "What am I expected to do around here?" They are tough questions, because the profession itself has not answered them; therefore, there's little help available to the communicator who begins questioning his or her role. They are also tough because management in general doesn't know what to do with communication professionals or how to manage them.

Largely in self-defense, communication people have solved the problem by developing an intense dedication to the communication craft and to its end products—brochures, product literature, audiovisual materials, house publications, and the like. Being defined as, and defining themselves as, writers, editors, producers, and reporters, that's what they limit themselves to in the organization. For their part, senior management can't understand why they need media people in their own organization. Or if they do see the need, they often regard them as one more group of service people like the draftsmen or reproduction department.

In fairness it should be noted that communication people have found this media focus more in desperation than by design. Frequently, I lead planning workshops for professional communicators as part of my consulting work. The workshop always begins the same way. I ask the group to share with one another the kinds of job problems that are uppermost in their minds. The list hardly varies from workshop to workshop.

Practically all the complaints have to do with the way they are managed —or perhaps better said, neglected. Heading the list is the complaint that they have ill-defined jobs. No one ever oriented them or told them the standards of success for their work. They were merely shown to a desk, perhaps apprenticed to an older practitioner, given back copies of publications, and told to go to work.

Following that casual introduction to the job, they find later that they have little or no access to their preoccupied senior people. They complain that what few meetings they have with senior people are perfunctory sessions in which they are told what and how they will communicate. Rarely are they asked for their suggestions or opinions, except on such mundane matters as style or punctuation.

A further complaint is that there is no direction given to their work. When their activities are directed, the direction is usually for a one-time situation that is a product of some kind of crisis. This crisis orientation, they say, is compounded because they get little or no support from their immediate bosses. That charge usually springs from the reluctance of their senior management to speak frankly to the issues. In too many cases, any attempt to produce this kind of communication in the name of the organization gets killed by a nervous aide, vice-president, or middle manager, and there is no route of appeal.

Of all the complaints I hear in the profession, this is probably the most typical. "I just don't believe that my management is interested in real communication. They say they are, but every time there is a serious matter that should be addressed they lose their nerve. I just don't believe them anymore." The result, of course, is that the communication people produce a typical house organ with the usual quota of such safe news as the standings of the softball team, the engagements, birthdays, and pictures of new employees and retirees, ad nauseam. At least this is what the lazy and dispirited ones do.

The good ones strike some sort of reasonable compromise and do the best they can in a difficult situation, settling for small victories. Or they leave for greener pastures. Or they become a thorn in the side of their own management. Given that their management really does need help and really does need to do better in employee communication, none of these alternatives is very attractive.

This is the perspective of the people who are trying to shape and often lead employee communication efforts. The senior executives who hire, manage, and evaluate communicators complain that such people do not understand the realities of business. They see them as naive and Utopian and frequently self-righteous about such matters as employee rights and the alleged right of people to know what is going on in the company. In many cases, management has real doubts that there is such a right to know and resent anyone telling them that there is.

The main complaint of such senior management is the lack of understanding or concern that communication professionals seem to have about the business and the risks of managing it, not the least of which is the risk of communicating. Often frustrated in their efforts to create the kind of understanding and commitment they see in other disciplines to the business' bottom line, they decline to take their professional communicators seriously and use their talents sparingly, badly, or practically not at all.

What seems to be required is some way to get institutional leadership and their communication professionals together in a frank discussion of mutual needs. For this to happen, senior management must first see the possibilities as well as the risks of good communication. Then they must believe in the skills of the communication people they employ. Because organizational c. mmunication today is almost purely reactive, it is hard for management to see much more than the risks. And ironically, management's concentration on the risks of good communication makes it less likely that they will ever acknowledge the possibilities. The answer seems to be to make a conscious attempt to make good proactive issues communication the main communication mode of the organization.

On the matter of skills, many of the people employed as organizational communicators are very bright, inquiring, well- trained technicians. Therein lies one of the profession's main problems. With poor or marginal direction, with low accountability, and with little exposure to the values, needs, and attitudes of their own leadership, they focus on the thing they understand best—their craft. This is fine if it's craftsmanship that the organization needs. In today's world, I doubt that. I believe what is needed is imaginative formulation of issues, the ability to see the organization's broad needs, and the willingness to join forces with any other organizational specialists to address the complexities of employee and public communication.

The ideal solution is the creation of a department of such people who report high enough in the organization to have the access and contact they need with senior people. But one of the major problems here is that such specialists too often are strange bedfellows. The personnel people—at least the bad ones—are too often cautious bureaucrats who thwart good communication on the grounds of risk. The public relations people—at least the bad ones—are too often reactive communicators and journalists who see themselves as the organization's media barons, wheeling and dealing with the press or producing slick internal media that no one has much faith in.

Perhaps the only answer here is the same as it is in most such situations. Senior management has to seek the best leadership it can for its communication arm, staff it with the most flexible and broadest people it can find, and then support it with the will to communicate in the face of all the risks and hazards that go with good communication. Indeed, of all these, perhaps the one essential ingredient is this one of will. Good communication sometimes is a painful process whose outcome seems forever in doubt. It's an activity that is certainly not for the fainthearted.

To see some of the real-life situations that these circumstances can produce, let's look at another fictional company and a typical communicator in today's organizational world—Gretchen Greensleeves. Greensleeves is 26 years old and has recently left her position with National Bank, where she was editor of the bank's monthly publication, *The National Banker,* a publication typical of the house organ breed. It carried to its 3000 readers the standard quota of president's messages, know-your-benefits columns, boring articles on the workings of the

Federal Reserve System (as plagiarized from various banking publications), a list of employee birthdays, and classified ads of employee property for sale or trade.

Greensleeves had been given the job as editor mainly because she was an overqualified secretary with a degree in English and a year's teaching experience. With the press of affirmative action targets at National Bank, she became a likely candidate for promotion. She knew how to spell and had a "flair for writing," and the job was open. So she was given the offer, which she quickly accepted to escape the tedium of clerical work. The only trouble was that she knew nothing about publications and less about the employee audience at National Bank.

But thanks to her "flair," the choice of a good quality printer who sympathized with her inexperience and needed the account, and management's not having any particular expectations for the publication anyway, she did well. She even won a couple of prizes for writing and design. Never mind that in her two-year tenure the tellers organized themselves into a union, secretarial turnover skyrocketed because of workload pressure, and middle managers barely communicated anything about anything to their people. For her part, she put on a successful poetry contest, collected and published some great recipes, and learned how to operate a camera for the grip-and-grin photos she regularly published. But it was not poor Greensleeves' fault that things were going so badly in the management and morale of the bank; it was just that she kept writing about the National Bank "family" all during this time.

In later years she would be amused by the irony of the situation, but the reaction she had after two years was frustration and disappointment. She decided that she wanted no more of the Kafkaesque situation at National and began looking for a job. As the scene opens, she has been hired as editor of the *Acme Recorder* as part of an extensive upgrading of the employee communication function at Acme Chemical Company. Acme is one of the country's leading chemical companies, employing 20,000 people in one large facility, where it is almost totally centralized both geographically and philosophically. The company was founded in the 1890s and for years has dominated its marketplace.

Paternalism runs rampant at Acme. Pay and benefits are good, and layoffs are unheard of, but this tranquil picture is now being threatened by chemicals being produced overseas and aimed straight at the Acme market at a lower cost and with aggressive sales and pricing. Alarmed by the new competition, Acme management has hired Ted Forrester as vice-president of communication. Forrester's job is to update the communication program at Acme and to wake people up to the threat that their company is facing.

Forrester has selected Greensleeves because she has recently lived through two years of poor communication practice, apparently has learned the lessons, and is anxious to begin tackling a real communication job. She is smart, hardworking, and has some solid ideas for improving the *Acme Recorder*.

For his part, Forrester has three main goals for employee communication at Acme. First, he wants to reverse the traditional close-to-the-vest communication posture so that people will understand the company's emerging problems and priorities—especially the new international competition threatening the Acme leadership position in the marketplace. Second, he wants to give Acme people a greater sense of urgency about such issues as productivity and government regulation of their industry. Third, he hopes to influence the internal culture of Acme so that people will be less complacent and so that Acme as a whole will be less paternalistic.

He recognizes that this is a tall order and has begun developing several media to put out his message to Acme people. He is especially interested in getting Acme managers to do a better job than they have in responding to the concerns raised by their people. The managers are a fiercely loyal and older group who believe that the company should not have to cater to these young people who don't want to give a day's work for a day's pay. In general they are intolerant of any criticism of the company. Not long ago, the local newspapers took the company to task in a series of editorials on Acme's waste disposal practices. The foremen's association drafted a response and urged its members to write letters to the editor asking whether the community wanted jobs or to give overseas competitors still greater advantages by upsetting Acme's cost structure by making them spend money for better waste disposal. The tone of the letters generally was how can you be so ungrateful to a company that has taken such good care of all of us, not to mention this community?

Greensleeves' first assignment in her new job is to interview the director of manufacturing. Of all the Acme managers, he is perhaps the most conservative and resistant to change. Greensleeves is anxious to do the piece on the Acme waste disposal policy and practices, a portion of the business under the director's direction. The man's name is Ed Bowes, and he has been with Acme for 38 years.

What Gretchen does not know is that Bowes is deeply concerned about the new communication program which Forrester has recently sold to Fred Eaton, Acme president, and which he presented recently to the senior staff. Bowes' reaction at the time was to attack these half-baked ideas about open communication. He was particularly upset about the changes planned in the *Recorder,* since he held that his people liked to get their name and picture in the house organ. When he heard that the publication was to be used to communicate work issues, he was aghast. "All my people want to do is come to work and do their jobs and go home and have a couple of beers and watch some television. Why on earth do you want to send that kind of stuff into their homes and upset them about issues they never thought about? We've had the *Acme Recorder* for 44 years. Why is it no longer good enough all of a sudden? What I believe is what my old Pennsylvania Dutch relatives used to say, 'If it ain't broke, don't fix it.' "

Greensleeves appears in Bowes' office exactly 10 days after he has listened to the Forrester presentation and voiced his personal reaction. She begins by outlining her plan to do the waste disposal story, saying there is considerable public concern as well as employee uneasiness regarding Acme's disposal practices. She tells Bowes she thinks Acme people have a right to know and that they could even help spread the word in the community about Acme's practices being safe and responsible.

Bowes, who has a short fuse anyway, looks at the woman in amazement. "Do you know how delicate an issue that is? None of our people give a darn how we handle our waste disposal problems. Why do you want to get them all worked up about something 99 percent of them never even thought about? I am flatly opposed to this, and I'll tell Forrester that as soon as I see him. We can't go shooting off our mouths about every little thing that goes on here. What would happen if the press got hold of this? They'd probe and question and check. Are you going to answer their questions if they do? I sure don't want these people in here asking questions that are none of their business. No interview. No story. And that's final."

When Bowes sees how disappointed Greensleeves is at his reaction, he softens slightly. "But I can give you a tip for a good story for the *Recorder* anyway. There's a woman over in Building 24 who has a great china doll collection. She's one of the best-known doll collectors in this part of the country, and I know for a fact that she's wanted to be interviewed by the *Recorder* for a long time. Stop by my secretary's desk on the way out, and she can give you the details. They're old friends."

Greensleeves is crestfallen as she listens to Bowes and senses all of Forrester's and her plans going up in smoke. It sounds like National Bank all over again, and she is obviously dejected as she recounts her experience to Forrester and warns him that Bowes will be calling him to put an end to the project.

Forrester listens sympathetically and tells Greensleeves that he hadn't planned on her going to Bowes as quickly as she had. He apologizes for not having included her in his early planning activities and tells her that he believes that the situation can still be saved. The problem is that Bowes is worried about the local press with all the bad coverage other chemical companies have been experiencing over their waste disposal. He doesn't want to invite any examination of Acme practices at all. Forrester wants to include waste disposal as one of several issues that he feels Acme must address with its own people and the public at large.

Although Greensleeves' call on Bowes has tipped his hand a bit before he's ready, Forrester believes that the situation can be saved. He and Greensleeves make an appointment with Bowes to discuss the matter and to determine if they can get his approval to do some research on the subject.

When they first meet with Bowes a week later, he is evidently angered that they are pursuing an issue that he thought he had closed off. Forrester lets the director ventilate his concerns and then makes an earnest plea that he listen to their proposal. Bowes agrees with evident impatience as Forrester tells him that they want only to do an analysis of the issue and of Acme practices now and in the foreseeable future. He promises that they will print nothing, that the research is for their own information, and that they will share their findings with Bowes. At that point they will judge if there is any benefit at all in doing a story for the *Recorder.*

"I don't care if you do the research," responds Bowes. "But if you print one word on this in the *Recorder,* I'll personally see that you are in hot water with Fred Eaton. I don't see how anything good can come out of it. And I see lots of possibilities for bad outcomes."

"Fair enough," answers Forrester. "We'll be back in a couple of weeks with some facts and recommendations for you to look at."

In the intervening two weeks, Forrester and Greensleeves spend most of their time doing four things. They research the objections of the environmentalists and other activists who have raised an outcry against the industry's disposal practices. They carefully research Acme practice now and in the last 30 years. They talk to the waste disposal experts in Acme to determine what their plans are for the future. And they put all this information together in an action plan for waste disposal communication.

They discover some interesting things. Until 1960, Acme was not terribly cautious about disposing of waste chemicals and products. Most waste went into landfills, but, fortunately, the landfills were in remote areas that never were developed. Acme engineers have monitored these areas in recent years, and there are no evident problems. They have reported their landfills to the State Environmental Commission and are voluntarily complying with all the current regulations on such areas. They have also bought any such land they can identify so that no one in the future could ever inadvertently develop it for any other use.

Acme engineers are also working closely with disposal experts to develop safe and economical techniques for any waste product they currently produce in their manufacturing operations. It is clear through all Forrester's investigations that Acme is doing its best to behave responsibly. Practices are monitored carefully; plans are in place to be certain that Acme not only complies with the law but also is well ahead of any legislation or other government regulation on the subject.

With all this in hand, Forrester and Greensleeves meet with Bowes. Based on their research, they have roughed out a special issue of the *Recorder* to express Acme's concerns about the issue and to outline all the programs and plans Acme has been pursuing to meet its obligation to handle waste disposal responsibly.

The stories are balanced to show that Acme, like other companies in the business, did not always understand the full implications of some of its practices but that it is moving as fast as it can to be sure there will never be any local environmental accidents or damage through Acme practices. When he sees it all put together, Bowes is impressed at the positive tone of the report. Although he was prepared to say no after looking politely at the proposal, he begins cautiously asking some questions about how they might handle such communication. The outcome of the meeting is that Bowes promises to look at the material and give a firm decision in a week.

In that time he consults with some of his peers. The reactions to the material are predictably mixed, but the consensus is that the report could answer some real concerns of Acme people and could help them in their own discussions in the community if the issue is raised.

After a week of agonizing and nit-picking the final copy, Bowes agrees to its publication. He even authorizes an advance release of the special issue of the *Recorder* to all Acme managers with a cover memo over his signature stating that he thought that they would like to see what Acme was doing about the crucial problem of chemical waste disposal. The advance copy is well received by the managers, several of whom tell Bowes that they plan to use it as grist for upcoming staff meetings.

What are the lessons in the continuing saga of Gretchen Greensleeves? For one, both Greensleeves and Bowes learn something about organizational communication.

Greensleeves discovers that the corporate process is often one of consensus and that, although a story may have merit, it won't be told until senior management is confident that the risk is acceptable. What Greensleeves may regard as an acceptable risk from her limited perspective may be assessed differently by the person who is actually accountable for the outcome of the problem.

Bowes finds that although there are risks in communication it can well be that the greater risk is to pretend that a situation does not exist or that no one has noticed it. This is a terribly naive position, but it's amazing how often accountable managers would like to believe that they are totally in control of information—if they don't talk about the matter, no one will. This assumption ignores the media and its tendency to probe and dig at the first sign of any reluctance to talk. And even more dangerously, it assumes that the grapevine simply doesn't exist.

As a practical matter, the good organizational communicator understands these management fears and prepares the way for the difficult story. He or she informs management well in advance of any work on the subject, gets agreement that the problem is real and will not go away, and wins consent to develop a story treatment to be communicated in the appropriate internal or external media. With this kind of groundwork, the approval problems generally are limited to agreement on the copy. In most cases this is still not an easy process, but it is far better than the technique of surprising the boss with a message that scares him or her into a knee-jerk reaction of "I don't want to talk about it. Ever."

For Gretchen Greensleeves or anyone else to behave the way I have described, however, the person has to understand his or her proper role in the organization. Organizational communicators are not paid to be independent journalists. They must help management state its position truthfully and persuasively. And if they can't perform this task for reasons of conviction or because of personal reservations about the position itself, they should do the honorable thing and resign. The trouble with most of us is that we want it both ways. We don't want to endanger our own security or muddy our consciences with ethical considerations about mouthing positions we don't believe. So we declare ourselves intellectually neutral and pose as journalists.

Not long ago I was delivering this particular sermon to a group of communication professionals, one of whom was a middle-aged man and (as I later discovered) an ex-newspaperman. The man challenged my vision of the emerging role of the organizational communicator on the grounds that what I suggested would "reduce us to the level of mere human relations specialists." In his remark and in his tone of voice was the implication that journalism is a holy calling and hiring on as a paid communicator is prostituting oneself.

That simple dichotomy is ridiculous, but it represents a spiritual struggle for lots of people I've known during my years in the communication profession. In large measure it stems from so many people entering the profession through the back door of the establishment they serve. They began as newspaper reporters, teachers, or writers, and when that didn't pan out, they began searching for a more lucrative living. A job as a company editor or as a public relations writer seemed to be a good out. Or perhaps they trod the same path as Gretchen Greensleeves. Whatever the career path that led them into communication, they are rarely very well prepared to sort out the subtleties of this question of the proper role for an organizational communicator.

Nor are the colleges and universities much help. Anyone who makes a conscious decision to become an organizational communicator will be hard pressed to find a program that matches the real-world responsibilities he or she will be expected to perform on behalf of the management. The professors of journalism tend to train people mainly for newspaper careers, not surprisingly. The trouble is that this is an occupation with limited career opportunity and even more limited remuneration. The professors of communication, on the other hand, tend to train academicians who can analyze and measure human communication tendencies and map communication relationships, and the like, but who have little understanding of the needs, goals, and priorities of a profit-making organization. In fairness, the situation is improving as universities begin to recognize opportunities for their graduates in institutional communication and in public relations, but the training is still geared to reactive communication almost exclusively. And in the worst cases, it is geared to house organ publication and the press flackery of an earlier era. But there are lots of hopeful signs in university programs here and there that it will soon be possible to find an undergraduate program turning out qualified people who understand to some extent what they are getting into.

For now, however, the organizational communicator is largely left to his or her own devices to learn the business. The lucky ones will work for someone who has the skill, insight, and patience to train them properly. The less fortunate will have to figure out for themselves what is expected and how to do it.

Thanks to the efforts mainly of the International Association of Business Communicators (IABC) and the Public Relations Society of America (PRSA), in-service training is becoming the most promising training alternative for the serious organizational communicator. Both organizations offer job-related training from people who are expert in the business and who have made their marks in their own companies. These workshops, seminars, and professional meetings offer people the invaluable opportunity to talk to people who may feel the same sense of isolation that they do.

Compounding the isolation issue is the matter I alluded to earlier in this chapter about where the communication function should report. Whether it is in public relations, public affairs, personnel, or some umbrella organization that includes part of all these probably does not make much difference *if*—and this is a crucial if—the function gets the management access, support, and ownership it needs to do the job. When it does get all that and when management displays the essential element of the will to communicate, communication people have a remarkable and exciting opportunity. They are then in a position to influence the very climate and tone of the organization tney serve. I can think of few other specialties in the organization with this kind of power.

Communication professionals can recommend communication initiatives and actions that help shape the nature of the business; then they can interpret the reality of those actions so that people can see the intent as well as the practices of the organization. In a word, they can begin to provide *meaning* to the day-to-day work life of people in the organization. If they do that well, they also begin to engender a sense of hope to those same people for their own futures as well as the future of the company. I don't mean to rhapsodize about all this, but where else in a work organization can you be in the meaning and hope business?

To see how a communicator can achieve this kind of professionalism, take a look at Sandy Kent, the editor of a monthly magazine for a national drug company called Apex Drugs, another fictional company. Kent is a skillful writer who began her career as a free-lancer. Married to an engineer, she soon tired of the uncertainties and rejections of free-lance writing and began looking for "a regular job." Because she is outgoing and bright, she impresses the hiring manager at Apex, Fred Seager, and he picks her to edit the company magazine.

In this, her first job in a business organization, she has some difficulty understanding the protocol. She is a young woman—barely 26—who has been brought up to believe that if you need to talk to someone, you call and make an appointment and go talk. That's exactly what she tries to do at Apex, a stuffy company in which the executive secretaries she calls give her a cold reception and reluctant appointments. When she begins to do interviews for the magazine, she also finds some of the male executives she's interviewing either are patronizing or give her a quick brush-off.

The first story she attempts to write at Apex is a disaster. She has decided that a good way to start would be with an article on employee compensation. To research the piece, she tries to compare Apex wages with other large drug companies. She even manages to break this data out by broad job categories and to make comparisons that way. Most of the data is very favorable to Apex, but there are a few spots where there are some slight variances between Apex wage rates and the competition. These are so small that they are inconsequential. Apex personnel people, however, are nervous about the whole subject and are using the "inequities" to attempt to kill the story.

Personnel's opposition, however, is ambivalent, since it originally agreed that such an article could go a long way toward helping Apex people understand what the company is doing to keep them abreast of inflation and how that is affected by the economics of the industry in general. When given a copy of the article for his approval, Dan Stokes, Apex personnel manager, takes a meat ax to most of it. He doesn't want to include any discussion of how salary grades are determined at Apex, stating that this is confidential. And he is especially nervous about implying that Apex can go on indefinitely raising salary grade maximums to keep up with inflation.

When Sandy gets the story back mutilated by the sometimes unkind and acid comments of Stokes and three or four of his staff people, she is demoralized. Most upsetting of all is that about a third of their comments are simply about matters of style. Stokes and his staff have even attempted to rewrite whole paragraphs to substitute their stilted phrases and professional jargon for the clear language she had chosen to explain some of the technical aspects of compensation policy.

Sandy's boss, Fred Seager, decides to see if he can save this piece on the grounds that personnel said in the beginning that it needed such a story to put to rest some of the misunderstanding of Apex compensation policy. In fact, the most recent attitude survey showed that there was considerable dissatisfaction with salary when, in fact, Apex rates were among the most generous in the business.

What Sandy is facing here is really the organization communicator's moment of truth—that bleak moment when he or she sits at the desk with several marked-up approval copies, some of which conflict with one another, and has to put it all back together again. It's a painful and deflating moment when all feelings of pride of authorship have to be submerged and the writer has to get on with the job of producing the article that will finally pass muster with the people or person who will be the final approval source. It is the moment that separates the professionals from the petulant, the open-minded from the close-minded, and the dedicated from the uncaring. Only those with a healthy sense of perspective—and humor—can survive this process year in and year out.

At this point, Seager decides to meet with Stokes to negotiate what he can and cannot tolerate in the story and why. He includes Kent in the discussion, but he handles most of the serious disagreement and forewarns her to keep her temper. Skillfully, he persuades Stokes to relent on some of his objections—those that are emotional and without any real substance. When there is a real issue and when the Apex case could be hurt or misunderstood, he softens the copy. In two or three passages, he takes points from the story because they raise more questions than they answer. The session is very instructive to Sandy, who watches Seager focus it on points of substance and reserve to himself the final decisions on style, all the time allaying Stokes' fears about the volatility of the subject.

At the end of the session, Kent and Seager have a very solid story that is well received by most Apex people. One of the most interesting pieces of feedback received when Sandy does the normal readership survey of the issue, a practice

Seager instituted some months ago, is that an overwhelming 98 percent of the audience read the entire story. Although there is some skepticism here and there, Stokes is surprised that he receives much favorable comment about the story.

From this early success, Seager and Kent begin to formulate other plans to address important company issues on the minds of Apex people. As one of their pet projects, they want to get Apex people into meetings with George Sideris, the president of Apex, and to improve upward communication through this device. They plan to have Sideris hold informal lunches or coffee breaks with groups of 10 or 12 people and to chat about the business. Sideris is a bit apprehensive when Seager and Kent first approach him with their proposal, but he agrees to try one session to see how it goes. But first, he wants some coaching about what Seager thinks might be on people's minds as well as some help with possible answers.

At the first coaching session, Kent is uncomfortable about coaching the president until she realizes that with all his presumed poise and knowledge, he doesn't know how to handle this situation. At that point she begins to relate more to him as a human being than as an authority figure. To make the session real, she roleplays the part of an angry feminist who is deeply distressed about Apex affirmative action intentions. She confronts him with all the toughest and most irreverent questions she can think of. By the end of the session, he has a worst-case example of what he might face, and he has handled it with candor and sincere goodwill. He is greatly relieved when the first such real meeting with Apex people is polite and enlightening for him as well as for those who attend.

In the feedback forms that Kent circulates to the audience after the sessions, she finds an overwhelming acceptance of the meeting. The positive responses to the survey questions are all in the 90 percent range. When asked if they want to see these kinds of sessions continued, the audience response is a 100 percent yes vote.

With this foot in the door, Seager and Kent are taking the first step down a long and bumpy road in which they will slowly help Apex management communicate more effectively with the work force. The victories will be small; the frustrations will be large sometimes, but Seager and Kent will make steady progress in improving the communication climate at Apex.

The state of the art—if we may call it that—in employee communication has been primitive. In an older work organization in which words were mostly used to give orders to people whose job it was to carry them out, the communication process itself was simple and decidedly one way. In today's organization, talk, discussion, dialogue, relationship, and commitment are vital. They are the very essence of managing people productively.

We are beginning to wake up to that fact and to remedy some of our bad communication habits. We still have some time, but it's an opportunity that will not linger. If we don't understand the demands it imposes and if we don't pursue it as professional communicators and as management, the opportunity will simply pause, stare expectantly at us, and then resignedly walk away.

The recovery and continued health of our vaunted industrial machine may even hang in the balance.

Chapter 7

Life Beyond the Corporate Walls

The way we divide and organize the organizational communication task has always reminded me of the parable of the blind men. When asked to describe the elephant, each man naturally described it from his unique perspective and touch. So it is with the organization's communication needs.

In one large pharmaceutical company I am acquainted with, the communication organization is divided into several major departments. There is a director of investor relations, a director of public relations, a director of public affairs, a director of community relations, and a director of employee communication, all of whom report to a vice-president of corporate communication. Each of the directors is a bit like one of the blind men in his or her perspective.

Because the company communicates reactively, it is very much oriented to communication programs. Each of the directors has his or her separate programs to nurture and protect. The programs are finely tuned to respond to whatever message the company needs to broadcast at any particular moment. They are at their best when there is a significant event to communicate and at their worst when nothing much in the way of hard news is happening. It is the latter situation that makes them a burden and sometimes an embarrassment to all concerned. When nothing is happening, people have to "develop" messages to fill their pages because they seem to have a life of their own.

If you could interview the directors separately, you would soon discover that there was little or no consensus about the major issues in the company. There is a vague agreement on some of the problems the company faces, but practically every one of those problems is overshadowed in their minds by the particular tasks they must perform to feed their programs. The only person who seems much concerned about the whole communication task is the vice-president of corporate communication, and even he deals with his people as though their various programs were the most important consideration. He is naturally interested in content but tends to orchestrate the content to reflect what his boss, the president of the company, is concerned with. And that's where the process begins and ends. For the rest of his people, it's all nicely compartmentalized according to the particular programs they manage.

This company, in my experience, typifies the way most institutional organizations have defined and managed their communication efforts. It looks neat. The accountability seems to be well defined. The job descriptions are all carefully put together and graded according to a traditional hierarchy in which customers are left to the advertisers and sales people; the public media are seen as the most important and potentially troublesome public audience; the investment community is seen as a key constituency to be communicated with; and employees and the local community are regarded as important but less threatening.

In today's environment I think such an approach is about as parochial and ineffective a scheme as we could invent. I say this because the approach perpetuates two major fallacies. The first is that the organization's information programs take precedence over its communication needs—and that the task is mainly management of those programs. This is an acceptance of the means as ends in themselves and is all too common a failing in organizational communication.

The second fallacy is the belief that what counts most to any organization is the good opinion and understanding of the public at large. Favorable public opinion certainly counts for a great deal, but I believe that the employee audience, which is really akin to a family, is the organization's most critical constituency. If a husband or wife does a marvelous job of relating to everyone outside the family circle and is thought of as a model person but is ineffective or absent for the other members of the family, there will soon be difficulties in the family that will make a sham of the person's otherwise successful life. In our personal lives, we can't ignore the more intimate relationships while we focus on the casual relationships. If we do, all we will have left is the casual relationships.

So it is with organizations. If the employee relationship—the intimate relationship—is ignored, all the organization will have left is the more casual support of people who have no real stake in the business. If you doubt this, consider the number of organizations you know who do first-rate public relations but are bad-mouthed by the people whom they employ. At a cocktail party in his or her local community, such a disgruntled employee can undo the work of countless dollars spent on good community relations.

None of the foregoing is the same as saying that the casual relationship can be ignored. It simply means that the casual relationship is a less intense relationship than the one employees have with the organization and must be attended to in a different way and with a different emphasis. In my judgment, most organizations have tended to take their employees for granted and have spent their money and time cultivating external publics. A husband or wife who does that is courting disaster. So is an employer.

Once these priorities are put into proper perspective, I believe that the external communication task falls nicely into place. Like the treatment of internal communication, handling external communication becomes a matter of good proactive issues communication that, in turn, is a product of the organization's interactions with its world. The end is the ultimate communication of those issues to the audiences that count. It is not the creation of programs that generate lots of activity and give the appearance of real communication but not much substance.

In my judgment all of the organization's communication needs are cut from the same cloth. Despite attempts to organize communication into several specialties matched to the audiences the organization is trying to reach, the organization's actions, decisions, and plans are the common information that each communication specialty is trying to explain. That information obviously does not change from audience to audience. What does change is the intensity of interest and concern that any given audience may feel about the information.

This is the only valid argument I see for dividing the professional communication organization into specialties such as investor relations, public relations, employee communication, and the like. The role of these various specialists should be simply to examine that common body of organizational issues and information and decide what and how to communicate them to the appropriate audience. The crucial step that is too often omitted is for management and the communication professionals to agree on the organizational issues themselves. Again, like the blind men in the parable, everyone is left to his or her perception of the elephant. The failure to identify and articulate the vital issues of the organization dooms the communication effort to a formless and confusing message that generally makes reactive communication the only workable method of operation.

The alternative lies in the proactive communication model we looked at in Chapters 4 and 5. Table 7.1 shows that the model applies equally to external and internal audiences. A good organization assessment will also yield important information to potential investors, governmental agencies, the community at large, and potential customers. Indeed, if it is done with the proper thoroughness, it will identify these audiences and their stake in the organization.

A sound set of fundamental assumptions about communication will include these audiences and the potential benefits or risks of communicating with them. It will, of course, also take a position about their importance or lack of importance to the organization's ultimate goals.

The guidelines for communication that become part of the program strategy will develop further who these audiences are and how they should be dealt with. When these decisions are made (and only then), the communication programs that are vital to the overall effort should be identified and funded.

Under the heading "Content Strategy" in the model, it is vital to be certain

TABLE 7.1 PROACTIVE COMMUNICATION TO EXTERNAL AUDIENCES

Steps of Proactive Model	End Product
Organization assessment	Identification of the organization's major audiences
	Understanding of primary issues
Fundamental communication assumptions	Assertion of risks and benefits of communication to particular external audiences
Program strategy	
Communication guidelines	More specific identification of audiences and who should be accountable for reaching them
Communication programs	Program development and creation to reach key audiences
Content strategy	
Message platform	Defining of issues and rating of their importance to given audience (e.g., high, moderate, low)
Message execution	Tailoring of issues to a given audience and selection of best media for their delivery to audience
Evaluation	Selection of appropriate evaluation techniques

that the message platform, that is, the major issues the organization needs to communicate, is further defined and then analyzed in terms of their interest to a given audience. For example, the issues can be rated as being of high, moderate, or low interest to any particular one of the organization's audiences identified in the organization assessment.

When the message platform has been identified and its various issues analyzed in terms of their urgency for a given audience, the next step is to decide on an appropriate strategy of message execution. Just how will that particular issue be tailored to the audience? What are the best media to reach that audience?

Finally, how will the success of the effort be evaluated? Will it be surveyed? Will it be researched in some other way? Is it necessary to adjust the message or fine-tune it? These and other kinds of questions need to be answered and fed back into the ongoing proactive issues process.

The obvious advantage of this proactive process with external audiences, as with internal audiences, is that the organization is scrutinizing itself and its priorities and actions to determine the impact on the public. The organization then uses the information to formulate an initiative with whatever external audiences are of concern. That initiative makes a lot more sense than loading the information shotgun and firing it in the direction of those people who might possibly be interested.

The traditional approach of merely reacting to events, complaints, or charges makes the organization look defensive or apologetic or—worse—as if it is engaged in cover-up. It is an approach that ironically aids the efforts of those who raise questions or plant suspicions about institutional motives, even when those questions are baseless or irrational.

The obvious disadvantage of this proactive public process is that it is hard work, requiring careful and creative analysis as well as lots of educated guessing. Part of the great appeal of reactive communication is that it is so easy to wait for things to happen and then to rush to produce and distribute a message to explain the event. It is the stuff and the romance of reporting, pounding out the story on an old typewriter, racing to meet media deadlines, and then waiting breathlessly for public reaction.

This has obvious appeal to people who feel a kinship with their brothers and sisters in the media. But, as I have been trying to emphasize throughout this book, it is the wrong kinship. Although the planning and research process may be less romantic, it is the essence of how effective organizations attack their work. In today's complicated world, organizational specialists of any kind who choose to wing it usually help bring on disaster. Communicators are certainly not the exception to this rule.

Perhaps the best way to illustrate the proactive process as a way to reach an external public is to cite a case history from a real-life company where I was once employed as manager of public relations. It was a high-technology capital equipment company producing exotic systems for manufacturing processes that could only be carried on in a vacuum. In staff attempts at organizational assessment we determined that one of the most important external audiences for us to reach was the engineers and scientists who influenced the buying decisions for our vacuum systems, many of which carried a price tag of $100,000 or more. The engineer or scientist was usually the first link in a complex process that required the approval of several fairly senior people in any given company. The result was that the sales cycle could be and was often a confusing and frustrating process.

Once we had identified this group of technical decision makers as an important audience, our next step was to begin developing an accurate assumption about the possible benefits of communicating with them. The final communication assumption we made could be stated as follows: the scientist or engineer who will actually use our products is a vital, although only an initial, contact in the sales cycle. He or she will have to win the approval of his or her management for any sale to be completed. Part of the communication task is first to reach that initial decision maker and then to assist him or her in providing reasons why our products should be purchased in preference to the competition.

This assumption was then converted to one of our communication guidelines:

It will be the responsibility of public relations to develop a technical publications and publicity program to communicate our unique capabilities to potential users in the technical community. The means for this program shall be the usual technical publications and programs that engineers and scientists routinely consult.

This guideline ultimately was converted to an ingenious program in which we encouraged our own engineers and scientists to write and publish papers and articles highlighting the technical advantages of our equipment. In public relations we researched the best media for reaching our customers and then made a determined effort to interest the editors of those publications in publishing pieces signed by our own technical people. It worked like a charm, and we managed to place upward of 50 or more technical articles and symposium papers annually. In fairly short order, this publicity, coupled with our aggressive advertising, was getting lots of attention with the potential customers we had hoped to reach. In fact, it was not unusual to get a telephone call from an engineer in a company we had little idea might be interested in our products. The call frequently came from someone who had read an article by one of our engineers and wanted to discuss it further. The call, in turn, became a good sales lead for the sales person closest to the caller's location.

In time we became so sophisticated with this kind of communication that we persuaded the local engineering college to cosponsor with us a symposium on a new technology that we were deeply interested in and had already developed a product for. With the university's name and prestige, we managed to put together a meeting that included the best-known names in this specialty from companies in the United States and abroad. Three hundred engineers and scientists attended our first such symposium and were given the chance to tour our facility and look at our equipment.

After the meeting we published all the papers that were presented and sold a proceedings in a bound volume that prominently featured our company name and the name of our cosponsor. It was for us a public relations and technical coup that ultimately led to countless sales leads. And this was only one of several such conferences we produced. So much for the program stage.

The next part of the model is content strategy. In this particular example, the issue for us was the need to get our company known among engineers and scientists as the leading technological firm in this unusual business. These people were the initial contacts in the sales cycle but they had to have help in convincing their own management that our product was not only superior but also a wise capital purchase.

To make this happen, we had to find the right statement of our message and the proper communication channels not only to the initial decision maker but also to his or her management as well. What this meant in practice was that we supplied our sales people with reprints of the articles and papers in question for them to pass along to their management in their proposals and documentation. It's interesting that a good article in a decent technical magazine is often seen as kind of an editorial endorsement of the technology. Most editors would deny this and say that it's simply information their readers should know about, but that's usually the unspoken view of the reader. Besides the articles, of course, we also distributed our product literature, but it was our view that the literature was much more suspect than the article reprints.

Besides the article reprints, we also did our best to get the real decision makers to attend the various technical meetings we sponsored with others or that we put on in connection with trade shows. This was the best strategy of all, because it sold the initial contact and his or her boss simultaneously, if they were impressed with our technology and product.

Obviously, this is one small example of how the proactive model can be used with a given external audience. Following the same steps, it is possible to identify all the important constituencies for the organization and to develop a communication plan that addresses each one of them according to the major issues in the organization.

For this example, evaluation consisted of two measures. First, how successful were we in winning the subtle, third-party endorsement we were seeking? This came down to two concerns: How many articles, meetings, and seminars could we put together to reach which audiences of customers? And how much participation could we get from our technical people in supporting the sales effort in this way? Both these measures were very good in the case I cite here. With a small technical staff, we were publishing 50 or so first-rate articles and papers and sponsoring a half dozen large and small technical meetings. It was an excellent addition to our paid-space advertising and product literature.

The second measure was "How well were we really getting to the decision makers and influencing their buying decisions?" This one was more difficult to determine, but we found that our work was influential in the majority of our large capital equipment sales. And certainly it did important things for our reputation as the premier supplier of high-vacuum products.

There sometimes is a fine line between reactive and proactive communication that can be troublesome to the purists. My advice is not to waste much time worrying about fine distinctions but to attempt to be proactive most of the time. A good example of what I have in mind is an incident connected with the Three Mile Island nuclear accident. Public utilities communication people, like their counterparts in the oil business, are always subject to public suspicion and public animosity because their products strike straight at the consumer wallet and are viewed as must expenditures. With nuclear power there is the additional hostility of the organized opposition to expansion of the country's nuclear plants.

When the Three Mile Island accident happened, at least one upstate New York utility did a very smart thing. Clearly, it was reactive communication in that it was a response to an event, but it was proactive in that it could never have been pulled off without advance discussion and the willingness of management to take a communication risk. A day or two after the radiation leak was discovered at Three Mile Island, the upstate utility announced an open house at its own nuclear plant, with guided public tours and speeches by its senior technical people on the various safety features of the local plant. Both the public and news media were invited to attend and to address their questions and concerns to the utility's management.

In my judgment this was good proactive communication because the utility was willing to talk at a time when the temptation was to say nothing to invite attention to local possibilities of a similar accident. It was a calculated risk that would not have been possible without advance thinking about how to deal with such a situation. The speed of the utility's announcement and invitation served to disarm its more vocal opponents, who were able to make only a few dissenting —and not very disruptive—comments in the face of management's willingness to talk about their safety efforts and the value of the plant.

Did this action win over thousands of converts to nuclear power? That's very unlikely, because the subject is so complex and emotional. But the action did demonstrate a willingness to carry out a communication initiative when it would have been simpler for management to do its best to maintain a low profile. It did forestall suspicious inquiry.

This kind of initiative is easier when there is a proactive plan in place that gives people the confidence and direction they might otherwise be lacking if they are purely on the defensive. No one can handle crisis communication with very much confidence if the task is really to fend off embarrassing questions and say as little as possible. Unfortunately, in far too many contemporary organizations, that has become the main mission of the public relations people. In the long run this can only worsen the unhappy adversarial relationship that has developed between the media and business or between business and government.

The wise organization is one that habitually researches its audiences and selects the ones most important to its immediate and future success and then develops a well-considered strategy for communicating whatever messages need to be communicated to those audiences.

For proactive issues communication to happen there will have to be a very different vision of the organization's communication responsibility. There will also have to be a very different organization of that responsibility to encourage a holistic view of communication. Although the details are beyond my capacity, I would envision perhaps a new position of vice-president of human affairs. This would be an amalgamation of today's personnel or human resource functions with the public affairs function. In most fairly sophisticated companies today, public affairs is the function that groups all the various communication specialties such as employee communication, investor relations, public relations, and governmental relations.

It is sensible to group these functions together, because they get at the vital organizational question—How can we run a humane organization that interacts responsibly and intelligently with other institutions and with the major needs of our society? This question can no longer be left to chance. It must be researched, planned, and managed just as the other major responsibilities of an organization are.

Finally, it can be delegated in name to our future and imaginary new vice-president. But it will remain always one of the primary responsibilities of the organization's top leadership, regardless of who owns the title.

Chapter 8

Conclusion

No discussion of communication would be complete without confronting an issue that clouds practically everything I say or recommend in this book. I refer to the belief held by many influential people that the real secret of getting people to perform effectively is the judicious use of force—either the force of authority or intimidation.

This sentiment was once expressed to me by the senior communication officer of a large financial organization. I shared a cab with him one day en route to the airport, and we were comparing notes on communication and its role within the organization. He was mainly a media person, he told me, and had little confidence in the line manager's ability or willingness to communicate effectively. I told him that I disagreed and that I believed that we *had* to find ways to energize the line manager in his or her role as communicator.

He listened politely and, I could see, skeptically, to what I had to say. Finally, he said that he, too, had once held such hopes, that earlier in his career he had been a trainer and a behaviorist in charge of the company's management development program.

Later, when he was director of communication for his company, he was taken aside by his manager after several months on the job. The manager said to him that he had some good news and some bad news for him. The good news, he said, was that he liked him. The bad news was that he had 60 days to straighten out his performance and to begin behaving like "a real manager." I gathered that the charge was that he had been too soft on people.

I didn't press him for details, but he clearly spoke like a man who had seen the error of his ways and corrected them. As he reflected almost wistfully about his conversion, he concluded that his boss had done him a monumental favor by "holding a gun to his head" and threatening to can him if he did not mend his ways. This is how people perform, he told me, by having someone demand that they do so—or else.

This experience has stayed with me for a long time, and it epitomizes an attitude that the organizational world will have a difficult time shedding—as it must. Otherwise, I fear for our ability to compete effectively with Japan or any other society that knows how to capitalize on human imagination and dedication.

The scientific data to prove my belief that we can increase human productivity through good issues communication and intelligent and caring management still need to be gathered at this writing, but the inductive leap to that conclusion does not appear farfetched. Indeed, it's like the classic story supposedly told by Sigmund Freud about an east European Jew riding a train to his village.

> [He] observed in the train which was taking him home to his village a young man who seemed to be going there too. As the two sat alone in the compartment, the Jew, puzzled by the stranger, began to work things out: "Only peasants and Jews live there. He is not dressed like either; but still, he is reading a book, so he must be Jewish. But why to our village? Only fifty families live there, and most are poor. Oh, but wait; Mr. Shmuel, the merchant, has two daughters: one of them is married, but for the other he has been seeking a husband. Mr. Shmuel is rich, and lately has acquired airs, so he would not want anyone from the village for his daughter. He must have asked the marriage broker to find a son-in-law from a family he knows. This means that it would have to be one that had lived in the village but moved away. Who? The Cohen family had a son. Twenty years ago they moved to Budapest. What can a Jewish boy do there? Become a doctor. Mr. Shmuel would like a doctor in the family. A doctor needs a large dowry. The boy opposite is neat, but not well dressed. Dr. Cohen. But in Budapest, Cohen wouldn't do. Probably changed his name. In Budapest? To Kovacs—a name which comes as naturally to Hungarians as Cohen to Jews."
>
> As the train drew into the village station, the old Jew said to the young man: "Excuse me, Dr. Kovacs, if Mr. Shmuel is not waiting for you at the station, I'll take you to his home and introduce you to your betrothed." Replied the astonished young man: "How do you know who I am and where I am going? Not a word has passed between us."
>
> "How do I know?" said the old man with a smile. "It stands to reason."[1]

So it is, in my opinion, with the assumption that an organization fostering a more human environment is likely to be more productive and more effective than an organization which treats human values lightly. I take issue with my acquaintance who asserted that performance in the real world is more a matter of holding a gun to people's heads than it is anything else. I believe that the gun only makes people so nervous and preoccupied that their performance is riddled with fear and self-doubt. I have yet to see people give generously of their talents when they were living under the gun.

Until the empirical evidence demonstrates conclusively that it is not so, I prefer to believe what my experience has been telling me for the last 25 years: that everyone gains when managers take their communication responsibilities seriously and do the job conscientiously. A manager who does so is able to manage toward business results more effectively because his or her people know the mission and objectives of both the group and organization. He or she is able to liberate the creative potential of the group and enhance productivity because the group members believe their opinions and suggestions will be taken seriously.

He or she is able to develop and sustain a dialogue within the group and promote the always-difficult task of upward communication. In that process, and as a result of it, people will tend to trust the manager and the organization and to feel much less alienated than they do in traditional organizations. The likely results are much less lying and repression of conflict, less likelihood of third-party interventions in the management or communication process, and a heightened sense of cooperation and teamwork in the group.

Even the possibility of achieving something like this on a large scale should be enough to tempt institutional organizations to search for ways to make the manager an effective communicator. Given our history, it will not be an easy task, but it is difficult to see what there is to lose.

In fact, there is a host of potential gains for the organization from a small investment in more effective communication. It may be possible to create a climate in which people honestly feel that they can speak out without fear of retribution. It may be possible to motivate people to give management their best suggestions on cost effectiveness and improved ways of doing things. It may make it easier for people to accept difficult decisions because they understand their necessity. It may permit earlier identification of mistaken policy or inappropriate practice. And, finally, it may improve the organization's chances of outdistancing its principal competitors in employee climate, thereby improving its ability to recruit, train, and retain people and improving its overall effectiveness in the marketplace.

The foregoing is not merely wishful thinking. There is lots of evidence around us if we choose to examine it. Social observer Daniel Yankelovich warns of the perils of continuing to ignore that evidence:

> The work place is one of the most conservative of our institutions. It has been highly resistant to change, particularly in the successive waves of individualism that have swept over so many other areas of American life . . . individualism flowers for top-level executives . . . but all other employees are expected to conform to rigid rules of group behavior. On ceremonial occasions, obeisance is paid to them: "Our people are our greatest resource and we must pay attention to their needs," their leaders say. But in everyday life, attention is paid to everything but people—capital requirements, technology, material resources, management techniques, political pressures, cost controls and markets.

A better-educated work force refuses to accept the old alienations that past thinkers assumed were inherent in modern society. The employees' challenge is essentially constructive; and if it is properly understood and acknowledged, we may emerge with a better society as well as with a healthier economy.[2]

Thus the ultimate answer to the organization's nay-sayers lies less in research than it does in observation and common sense. When all else fails, we can say with considerable confidence, like the apocryphal Jew described by Freud: "How do I know? It stands to reason."

NOTES

1. Victor Zorza, "After Brezhnev. . . . ?" *Washington Post,* January 12, 1975.
2. Daniel Yankelovich, "The New Psychological Contracts at Work," *Psychology Today,* May 1978, p. 50.

The 40 Most Common Questions About Communication

In the years I have spent in the communication business and especially at communication seminars and workshops, I often hear and am asked questions about how the function should be organized and managed. Recognizing the infinite variety of institutional organizations that exist in our society and, therefore, the infinite variety of twists and turns each one of these questions might take, I have nevertheless attempted to put together a list of the 40 most common questions people ask about organizational communication. Here are my answers, which I warn you must be carefully filtered and adapted to your unique circumstances.

1. Question
I'm an editor of a company publication and would like to convert it from a typical house organ into a full-blown proactive communication program. Where do I start?

Answer
The first thing you should do is really understand the proactive communication model in Chapter 4. That will be your blueprint. Next, you should take a very careful look around your own company to find out where you might find some likely allies in other specialties. The most obvious one is personnel—especially the training or management development people. Tell them what you're up to and why, and try to enlist their aid. Once they have some ownership in the effort, together you can begin developing a proactive plan that has the support of at least two major functions. This makes the selling job to senior management easier. Try to convert the various phases of the proactive plan into a written proposal and then line up functional support for your proposal, but be sure that you don't invent this as the sole property of the communication people. That may seem like a good way to get credit for your work, but it will probably doom the proposal.

2. Question

I'm the president of a small company (500 people) and can't afford professional communication help. What should my communication priorities be?

Answer

The best communicator I've ever seen was, like you, the president of his own small company. What he did was rely mainly on face-to-face communication, with the emphasis on informality and removal of status barriers. He worked in his shirt-sleeves and toured the plant the same way. He spoke to people in a friendly manner and worked hard to understand their problems. He began every day by touring the facility and greeting his people. He knew what was going on. He also held employee meetings of all kinds, some in his office with people from the production line. In short order, his managers followed his example, and it was an excellent communication climate. For his external communication he relied mainly on an advertising-public relations agency, preferring to expend his personal energy inside. To my mind, those are the proper priorities. For the record, the employee publication was a modest once-a-month newsletter that highlighted business results and business issues.

3. Question

As communication manager, I know that there are serious attitude problems in our insurance company. But no one in senior management would fund attitude surveys—partly for fear of finding out how bad things are. How do I get over this hurdle?

Answer

What you report is not unusual. "No news is good news" is the view of those who suspect that there are attitude problems they don't want to hear about. Obviously, this is a short-sighted view, and sometimes it can be corrected by pointing out to people such telling statistics as those concerning turnover and union organizing attempts and, if records are kept, employee complaints. If you don't want to spend inordinate time fighting fires in your company, it's important to give employees an attitude survey at least once every three years. Otherwise, the complaints simply fester until they explode in some sort of eruption that catches everyone off guard. Usually that's when people want to do an attitude survey.

4. Question

If you had a limited communication budget, where would you spend your money? What would your priorities be?

Answer

The most expensive kind of communication obviously is print or audiovisual. The least expensive—in direct costs anyway—is face-to-face. I would put most of my effort and most of my money into fostering face-to-face communication. If I had any money left over, I would invest in modest publications and inexpensive strategies such as cleaning up the bulletin boards. Ironically, big communication budgets can lead to extravagant and slick programs that don't communicate nearly as well as a senior staffer meeting with his or her people and answering their questions.

5. **Question**

If you focus on the communication of business issues in your publications, how do you communicate news?

Answer

The truth is that news mostly takes care of itself, if it really is news. The grapevine, the news media, all the usual channels will be sure that news gets out. Issues, on the other hand, have to be shaped and considered and then communicated purposefully. In my experience, it's difficult to get most managements to communicate news at the point that it is news. The trouble is news doesn't have that nice beginning, middle, and probable outcome if it's truly news, and management does not want to say a whole lot about it because they honestly do not know how it will come out. Many companies have solved this problem with news bulletins they post on company bulletin boards at the same time that they make press releases on such things as reorganizations, new products, earnings statements, and the like.

6. **Question**

My management refuses to be candid with our employees. As the communication manager, what can I do?

Answer

First, you need to understand why there's this lack of candor. Does your management fear the communication process? Have they been burned by poor communication of a difficult subject? Do they think company information is nobody's business but their own? Do they naively believe that nobody cares or that everyone knows anyway? Or do they perhaps think by talking about difficult matters they will raise concern where it doesn't already exist?

My experience is that management fails to communicate for some or all of these reasons. The best antidote I know of is a good proactive communication program. If that's unthinkable to your management, you may have a lip service job, and I urge you to reflect on whether you should polish up your resume. But first be sure you understand the nature of your management's reluctance.

7. **Question**

How high on the priority list would you rate shareholder communication?

Answer

That's really a "compared to whom" question. Obviously, shareholders are an extremely important constituency to any public company, because they are the owners and the source of capital. But I suspect that most shareholders just want some reassurance that the company is protecting their investment properly. A good, clear annual report, perhaps a well-done quarterly publication of some sort, and an informative shareholder meeting should take care of the need nicely. I part company with those who would tell shareholders more than they really want to know—those who argue, for example, that anything you give to employees you should also distribute to the shareholders. I believe that's overkill.

8. Question

Does economic education for employees make sense?

Answer

If you mean education in the basics of the private enterprise system, I cast a resounding no vote.

The best economic education anyone could get comes from daily life. In recent years we have all learned about inflation and productivity decline as we never could have learned from an economics course.

If we want to teach the private enterprise system, let's do it through good issues communication about our own organizations. In that context the lessons matter. Out of that context, they are an excellent example of a solution in search of a problem.

9. Question

My management wants to urge our employees to write to our various legislators in support of company positions. Does that make sense?

Answer

Not unless the position is one that matters to employees. Some people are now looking at employees as a great potential lobby of concerned citizens who can be counted on to support the company's positions on various pieces of legislation. I doubt that. Most employee audiences are smart enough to see through a communication program that is highly politicized. An employee's first question is "What does all of that have to do with me?" The second is "After all these years, why the sudden interest in my letters and my vote?" The fact is that employee identification with the company's cause has to be earned, not simply summoned.

10. Question

What is the impact on the communication effort when employees are unionized?

Answer

Because a union is a third party, it always complicates communication. The existence of the union means that at some point someone badly screwed up in communicating with employees. Otherwise, there would be no need for a union. Once the union is there, the wise management makes peace with it and keeps it a party to the need for good communication by informing its leadership and membership of company plans, problems, and intentions. The trouble is that if the company does this really well, the need for union representation becomes less and less evident. Most labor leaders would prefer to see senior management withhold information or communicate it badly. Then it is clear why a union is needed.

11. Question

Television and other audiovisual techniques are being touted as the best way to communicate with today's television generation. Are they really superior to print communication?

Answer

More and more, I'm in the minority among communication professionals on this subject. But I say no. Television is a terribly unforgiving medium. The audience for our television efforts is used to network quality performances. When we give them amateur night at the

Bijou, I think we hurt our management more than we help. It's one thing for a senior person to be a remote name on an organization chart. It's another thing for him or her to be a talking head with a slight tremor in his or her voice, all the time staring straight at the camera, unable to blink. Slide-tape presentations, and the like, are a little better received, but where do we find time in the work schedule to assemble everyone in a darkened room to watch what can only be seen as a message from Mount Olympus?

Print media, on the other hand, are compact and portable and can be read with minimal expenditure of time and energy. They can also be reread to catch what was missed the first time through. On top of all that, they're a lot cheaper.

12. Question
Can a consultant really see things I haven't seen as the professional communication manager? Does it make sense to hire one to analyze a company's communication problems?

Answer
It depends. If you understand your organization and your job, there probably won't be too many surprises in what a good consultant will tell you. And, if you think about it, there shouldn't be. On the other hand, the outside expert can be an important ally in persuading your own management that the problems are potentially serious. And the good ones will always identify a few things that you have missed or that you perhaps saw differently. In short, a good consultant is well worth it. But be careful. There are as many pretenders in consulting as there are in any other profession.

13. Question
What about upward communication? What works best?

Answer
In my judgment, the very best upward communication device is a good attitude survey in which results are compared with appropriate national norms. Such a survey not only identifies the trouble spots but also gives people a chance to talk to management about corrective actions. Done well, it can be a very useful tool. Done badly, it can make things even worse than they were. The worst thing, of course, is to ignore what people say or dismiss it. In that case, it would be better if the survey were never done.

Next to the attitude survey there are several anonymous communication programs that permit written or telephoned comments to management. These are then answered privately or publicly or both. If the employee comments are answered honestly and responsively, this kind of system can be an important adjunct to the normal manager-subordinate relationship.

One of my own favorite forms of upward communication is any meeting permitting employees to meet with the boss and get their concerns on the table. These can be held in groups as large as 50 with good results. Naturally, the smaller the group, the better the dialogue is likely to be.

14. Question
Don't the personal items in the company publication increase readership? Things like new employee pictures, employee activities, hobbies, and the want ads? People tell me that's what they like to read.

Answer

It all depends on the size of the organization. If it's small, those things can be useful in developing a sense of belonging. If it's large, they're just plain ridiculous.

In any case, they can never substitute for the substantial business issues that people need to understand to do their jobs better. Those are the reason for the publication's existence, not the want ads.

Also, be careful of what people tell you they like to read. The best way to find out this information is to use readership surveys to check what they actually do read.

15.   Question
Why should the harried line manager take the time and trouble to worry about face-to-face communication?

Answer
If a manager understands the job, he or she will acknowledge that in today's organization face-to-face communication comes with the territory. I'm convinced that much of our productivity problems today stems from a failure to recognize this need and pay proper attention to it in our planning, our execution, and our reward systems. Managers who claim they don't have time to communicate are clearly being rewarded for doing something else, and my guess is that the something else is not necessarily what the organization needs to have done as badly as it needs to have its people properly managed.

16.   Question
In an organization made up of decentralized businesses, where should the communication emphasis be—on the individual business or the larger organization?

Answer
Most surveys show that people have the strongest information need for what's happening in their immediate environment. Once this need is satisfied they are interested in the larger picture if that seems relevant to their work lives and experience. That's why it's so important for the boss to be a good communicator. In fact, you can have the slickest communication programs in the world, but if local management is messing up communication on a day-to-day basis, all those slick programs will be neutralized and rendered ineffective.

17.   Question
Shouldn't employees understand their relationship to the larger organization? Shouldn't they care about it?

Answer
In my experience employees regard home office operations as the remote "they" responsible for all the crazy and ill-conceived schemes they have to suffer. This attitude always upsets home office people, but it's a fact of life communicators can't change. Once we attend to local information needs properly, then and only then will employees be interested in the larger organization. This problem, incidentally, is compounded when the parent organization has a different name. This enhances employee disinterest.

18. Question

We spend several million dollars a year on our benefits program, but few of our people know much about how the program works. Attitude surveys tell us that the employees are satisfied with their benefits but don't know what they are or what they're worth.

Answer

About all employees want to know about benefits is that they are there when they need them and whom to contact for help with the forms and paperwork. Ideally, employees would also be appreciative of how much these programs are worth to them as well as what they cost the employer. I fear, however, that people tend to take such things as their common due. Therefore, I think routine communication about benefits is largely a waste of paper and ink. New benefits, of course, as well as benefit changes, do need to be communicated. But regular benefits columns will go largely unread. A benefits handbook of some sort is necessary, and lots of mileage can be obtained from an annual computerized benefits statement that tells people once a year on one sheet of paper what they have and what it cost the company. That's really about as much information on benefits as people can stand. If you hear lots of noise in your company about benefits, it's not that people don't understand what they're getting. Rather, it's that they don't like the program or consider one or more of its provisions inadequate. Rarely, if ever, can you talk employees out of these feelings.

19. Question

When there are difficult stories to communicate to the media, my management invariably wants not to communicate. How can I change that?

Answer

You probably can't for the simple reason that business leaders have become very gun-shy about the media. Your best hope lies in persuading your management that—like it or not —they are public figures and that there is public interest in what the company is doing and how it is doing. When they accept this, it is often useful to see that they are given some professional training in how to meet the media. Several consulting firms have begun to train people in presentation skills and in how to deal with an interviewer.

Beyond this, I would strongly recommend that an organization's external communication be made as proactive as possible. And this includes media relations. If the reporters know you and your problems to some extent, they are much less likely to come at you as an adversary. If they don't know you and your organization and you give them a cold shoulder, there is a good chance that they will adopt the adversarial role in reporting your problems and embarrassments. The stonewalling tactics practiced by Nixon's people during Watergate brought on exactly the kind of probing and digging that they were trying to prevent. This should be a good lesson to all who believe that a "no comment policy" can work.

20. Question

As a communication manager, I simply can't get access to senior management. What can I do to get them to recognize the needs I see?

Answer

One of the beauties of proactive communication is that it ties the communicator to his or her own management and forces a closer relationship. It also tends to stimulate management interest and support. Conversely, that is one of its weaknesses. If a closer relationship does not get established, proactive communication will probably not work.

In the situation you describe it is unlikely that you can get your management to see the needs you see. What may turn your senior management around is some sort of crisis that makes it crystal clear that something must be done to improve communication with one or more groups.

21. Question

Isn't one of the best uses of the employee publication recognition of employee accomplishments?

Answer

That is very often offered as the primary reason to establish an employee publication. My experience with readership surveys of what people actually do and don't read tells me that one of the least-read kinds of stories is the so-called recognition piece. People don't like to read about the glowing accomplishments of other people, contrary to popular opinion. I suspect that part of the problem here is envy. Another part is remoteness of the person. If the reader doesn't know the person written about, they're just not interested.

I think there are much better ways to recognize people than printer's ink. A warm thank you, a letter of congratulation from the boss, a luncheon with his or her peers, and, perhaps best of all, a substantial check or a promotion.

In brief, my experience says that one of the worst uses of the employee publication is for employee recognition.

22. Question

We have a slick employee magazine printed in four colors and mailed quarterly to both employees and shareholders. It's 10 years old, has won several professional society awards, and is a favorite of our management. The problem is that we can't afford any other publications or programs because of its cost and the staff time it absorbs. Is there anything we can do?

Answer

What has been created and is being nurtured is a monster. This happens in far too many organizations in which the appearance of communication is accepted as proof that the organization is indeed communicating. Mistake number one, in my judgment, is to issue such a publication only quarterly. That's not nearly often enough to address employee communication needs. Mistake number two is to send the publication to two very different audiences. I find it difficult to believe that one publication can hold two audiences with interests as different as employees and shareholders have. Mistake number three is to assume that because management likes the publication and because it has won writing or graphics awards that it is well received by its audience. And perhaps the most serious mistake of all is to allow that one publication to soak up most of your communication dollars and time.

I would commission some research to see how well this publication is serving the communication needs of your organization. To do that I'd recommend a thoroughgoing organization assessment, identifying both audience needs and issues, to see if this approach makes sense. My bet is that you'll find that you're squandering time and money and not really reaching either audience.

23. Question
If we eliminate the want ads and employee activities from our publication, won't we suffer a serious loss of readership? Who wants to read company propaganda?

Answer
If the most interesting part of your current publication is the want ads, you *may* suffer a readership loss. The challenge is to eliminate whatever in the publication is frivolous and useless and to replace it with what employees want and need to know. I believe that the formula for a successful employee communication program has its basis in the answers to these questions: Where is this organization going, and how will it get there? What does this mean to me? I'll take this kind of information any day in preference to want ads and bowling tournaments, and so will most people who are concerned about their work lives. If you present this material properly, your readership will not decline.

24. Question
Where do employees get most of their information today? Where would they like to get it?

Answer
Most surveys that I've seen say the number one information source in the company is the grapevine. When they are asked to rank the number two source, employees usually cite company publications. When they are asked to give their preferred source, they generally name the boss as their first choice, with the company publications second, and the grapevine way down on the list. The reasons are obvious. Employees know the boss and trust the information if it comes from him or her as the official source. Grapevine information is too often shaky about the details, although it can be remarkably accurate in forecasting forthcoming events.

25. Question
Are managers in most companies well informed about the subjects they should discuss with their people?

Answer
In general, we have not trusted managers in most organizations to communicate information to their people. I think most of us were traumatized by that old parlor game of passing a message from person to person and watching it get distorted. At least, that's the fear I usually hear expressed when someone suggests that the chain of command be used for communication of company information. Everyone is always afraid the manager will screw it up, embellish it, or even take issue with it. So they play it safe and communicate via a memo, a newsletter, or some other device that doesn't permit questions.

The result is that managers in most companies are not as well informed as they should be. But this doesn't mean they can't be brought up to speed and given the chance to communicate with their people. It just means that we use the situation as one more excuse not to trust managers to communicate information.

26.   Question

Given that managers are not as well informed as they should be, aren't media safer for important or complex communication?

Answer

Media have the appearance of being safer, but I think that's because it's difficult for people to challenge a piece of paper. If they don't like the message, misunderstand it, or are unhappy about it, there is no one to carry their concern to without the extraordinary action of writing a letter or asking for a meeting with someone in authority. This strikes most people as too risky, so they grumble to their co-workers, family, and friends. Senior management never hears the grumbling or writes it off as the view of malcontents and assumes that the communication has been successful. Meanwhile, morale sinks, and so does the company's reputation.

If we equip managers with clear information, supply possible questions that people might raise (together with some suggested answers), and give managers a head start on the grapevine, I'm confident that they would handle the communication task successfully. At the worst, the managers would do as well as the various written messages that we send off to people. At best, they might put a human face on an otherwise difficult-to-understand action and answer a few questions before they become gripes and suspicions.

27.   Question

What kind of formal training should a communicator have to understand his or her job?

Answer

For openers, he or she should be a good writer, for the simple reason that the main part of the job to date has been written communication. I am disturbed by the number of people today who seem to acquire a degree in communication without learning how to write or produce print media. It's nice to be able to produce a television program or a slide-tape show or to draw a diagram of the communication relationships in a group, but if you can't write clear, concise English, you won't get or hold a job in organizational communication.

Also, I have a liberal arts bias. Learn to write, learn some history and political science, learn some psychology, and learn to trust your ability to think clearly about difficult subjects. The rest you can pick up as you gain experience.

28.   Question

Would it be helpful for a communicator to get a master's degree in business to understand better what he or she is writing about?

Answer

I don't think that's particularly necessary or useful. You can learn what you have to know about most businesses in a relatively short time on the job. A good undergraduate course in economics should take care of the rest.

29.   Question

What personal qualifications should a good organizational communicator possess?

Answer

I would put at the top of the list the ability to deal with ambiguous situations. Very little in organizational communication is cut-and-dried. You have to invent your own job in many places and deal with a management that may even have hired you as the answer to its communication problems. It takes skill and time to develop a good working relationship with your own management and to make the programs you will be responsible for successful. A good communicator is like a long-distance runner. He or she has patience and tends to measure progress in small victories.

30. Question

Our company is small and can't hire a professional communication staff. Does it make sense for us to hire a public relations agency?

Answer

Before I did that, I would carefully examine the need. It may be that you can handle most of the problems yourself if you're small enough. If not, pick an agency that is likely to comprehend your unique need and give you personal service. Beware of boiler plate approaches that may have little to do with why you felt you needed communication help in the first place. You'd do better to suffer with your own amateur efforts than to resort to fill-in-the-blanks communication.

31. Question

My company has a long tradition of executive perks like special parking, private executive dining room, and an isolated and elaborate executive office suite. Does this hurt good communication? Is there a way around it?

Answer

Yes, I believe that it does get in the way. I also doubt that there are too many organizations which will wipe out such things, because they are too much a part of the system. Also, there are lots of people who have worked hard to achieve the position they're in, and they want the symbols that go with their achievement.

About the best we can do is work hard to neutralize the symbols. But there is no question that communication is less honest, more formal, and more difficult when people feel unequal and inferior. Maybe it's time to apply some of our cost benefit thinking to the whole subject of such status perks. Are they worth their cost in light of their adverse effect on good communication?

32. Question

As company president, I'm not sure that I trust my communication people to do my communicating for me. What do you say to that?

Answer

You shouldn't. No one should do your communicating for you. But you should get them to help, if they're any good. If you're not sure, find out. And if they're not good enough, get them some help or replace them. But be absolutely sure that you've given them your time and support in understanding what has to be done and in beginning to do it. Communication professionals are like any other staff people. They need guidance, and they need access to you. Nothing is worse than the little approval game that some senior people play in which they vaguely outline an idea and keep sending a writer back to the typewriter until he or she gets it exactly the way that the boss would have written it if there had been time. That's torture for all concerned. If you want exactly your own words, write it and give the writer the opportunity to do some light editing. Otherwise, understand that there are many ways to say the same thing, and don't insist on your way. And, finally, be patient. The mess we now have in communication is one we made together. Let's correct it together.

33. Question
I have no budget for consultants. Where else can I get the help I need?

Answer
One interesting possibility is your local university—if it has a good communication program or good human resource program. Occasionally, you can locate a bright professor who wants to give his or her students some good practical experience on real problems. Sometimes you can find a good match by bringing your problems for discussion and, then, if it's appropriate, giving the professor and students access to your people. The caveat, of course, is that you'd better supervise this kind of activity carefully. Other than that, read the experts and attend their workshops and seminars, and do it yourself.

34. Question
In my company the personnel department controls anything to do with managing our people. They'll never let me do anything to influence face-to-face communication—especially since there's a turf battle now because I handle employee publications and report to public relations. Is that a major problem in putting together a successful program?

Answer
It is unless you can find a way to bridge that organizational boundary. When part of the solution to the communication problem lies in one organization and part in another, someone has to put the parts together or the organization as a whole will continue to suffer. At this writing, the best solution would seem to be good teamwork across those organizational boundaries. The last thing you need is rivalry. Approach the personnel people and tell them of your interest, and offer your help in addressing the whole problem. Once you have forged that alliance, then go together to your respective bosses with a common proposal. It will be hard for them to say no to your desire to cooperate on a complex problem. Everyone believes in teamwork—at least in theory. Once the effort gets under way, make sure that it is an open secret and see how much attention it will get. If you do your work well, you will be surprised at how receptive everyone will be to your cooperative venture.

35. Question
Why are the media so unsophisticated about business? All they want to cover is the financial picture or the sensational stories. As a senior executive, it has made me very gun-shy about even talking to them. We're big in our middle-sized community, but I avoid the press like the plague.

Answer

I can understand your fears, but the best way to produce the bad press you worry about is to ignore the media people. There's a simple truth in the competitive business of reporting the news. If you don't give the press your story, it will make up one of its own by talking to your critics. It is a sure bet that you will like that story a lot less than any the press would have got from you—even if the news you have to report seems unfavorable. About the media's lack of sophistication about business, much of that is also our fault. When we do talk to them voluntarily, it is normally to report the financial picture. For the sake of the financial community, we present the most favorable results we can—sometimes with lots of hype. And then we turn to our other constituents and poor-mouth the same results. We can't have it both ways without confusing people as the least consequence or causing distrust as the worst consequence.

36. Question

I'm discouraged that in my personnel role I have to rewrite so much copy prepared by the communication people. They always change the language we have chosen so carefully for our statements to our people. I get so fed up with the approval problems and the need to change their copy back to its original form.

Answer

This one is classic and has its roots in the fact that everyone who can write a sentence or who took English 101 in college feels equally qualified to say the same thing equally well. If your communication people are skilled writers, then let them do what they get paid for —even if they change some of the words you attempt to carve in stone. It is an insult to sit down with a professional writer and review with him or her every word and phrase in a piece of writing so that you can share what you were trying to insinuate with this or that nuance or turn of phrase. The audience to whom you're directing the message is a collection of mere mortals who will reduce any message you give them to whatever they find believable and acceptable. The words you use will have minimal effect on that process of simplifying official messages. Opaque words chosen to protect tender egos or to cloud minds only worsen the problem.

If your people can't write clear English, then we have a different problem. If they can, then my advice is let them do it. After all, how would you feel if they took up compensation planning on the side? That's how they regard your attempts to convert English back to personnelese.

37. Question

As the president of a manufacturing company, I'm still not convinced that my people care about all these business issues. To them a job is a job is my belief. How do you react to that?

Answer

I don't question that different people work for different reasons. But in modern American society, there is practically no place where you go that someone doesn't invariably ask the code question: What do you do? It's a code question because we all know the question is a request for us to describe our occupation so that people can better size us up—our relative importance, how much money we probably make, and even whether we're worth their time and interest. For that reason alone, people regard work as central to their identity.

People who conclude that a job is a job do so because it has been made clear to them that only their labor counts. They feel their opinions, concerns, and ideas don't matter. At this point, they give up the ownership of anything but their labor and become merely workers—a flat-sounding word that describes a very demotivated and flat person. It also implies, I'm afraid, a self-fulfilling expectation.

38. Question
I'm not comfortable relating to my people in face-to-face company meetings. How do you handle the inevitable grandstanders and troublemakers?

Answer
In the last 15 years of running such meetings, I have seen that kind of behavior on only a few isolated occasions. Most people value the opportunity to ask the boss a legitimate question. They aren't foolish enough to blow that opportunity or to risk incurring the boss's bad opinion. Indeed, the real problem is to get people to *risk* asking the tough questions. The senior executive conducting such a meeting generally has to work hard in the beginning to make it clear that he or she wants and will answer tough questions.

39. Question
What about the lost productivity that results when you close down a work operation so that everyone can attend a meeting? I don't see how you can justify the loss of time.

Answer
If you assume that all work time is productive time, you may have a valid objection. But I think that most of us are not that naive. People in a work group can make up for lost production if they want to. One of the best ways to get them to want to is to treat them like interested members of the organization and to make a clear effort to keep them informed. There is a way to schedule employee meetings if we regard them as important. Imagine the opposition that must have been faced by the first person who suggested the idea of a quality circle! Yet in many companies, these meetings are becoming an accepted way of enlisting worker participation.

40. Question
Can you really expect managers to change their old habits and manage people in the way you seem to suggest? Isn't that asking too much?

Answer
I've heard at least one expert suggest as many as one-third of today's managers will not be able to manage successfully in the emerging organization environment, with its emphasis on good human resource skills over mere authoritarianism. I agree that it will not be easy for managers to understand the need to change the old ways, but I wonder if anyone really has a choice. Unfortunately, we have trained people well in the use of threat and intimidation in our various institutional organizations. Changing that culture will not be easy, but the need to revitalize our industrial complex and compete effectively in world markets should be enough to persuade us the change is at least necessary.

Index